The Story of
What Child Was This?

As Told in Scripture

(New Revised Standard Version)

Luke 2:1-20

In those days a decree went out from Emperor Augustus that all the world should be registered. This was the first registration and was taken while Quirinius was governor of Syria. All went to their own towns to be registered. Joseph also went from the town of Nazareth in Galilee to Judea, to the city of David called Bethlehem, because he was descended from the house and family of David. He went to be registered with Mary, to whom he was engaged and who was expecting a child. While they were there, the time came for her to deliver her child. And she gave birth to her firstborn son and wrapped him in bands of cloth, and laid him in a manger, because there was no place for them in the inn.

In that region there were shepherds living in the fields, keeping watch over their flock by night. Then an angel of the Lord stood before them, and the glory of the Lord shone around them, and they were terrified. But the angel said to them, "Do not be afraid; for see—I am bringing you good news of great joy for all the people: to you is born this day in

the city of David a Savior, who is the Messiah, the Lord. This will be a sign for you: you will find a child wrapped in bands of cloth and lying in a manger." And suddenly there was with the angel a multitude of the heavenly host, praising God and saying,

"Glory to God in the highest heaven,
and on earth peace among those whom he favors!"

When the angels had left them and gone into heaven, the shepherds said to one another, "Let us go now to Bethlehem and see this thing that has taken place, which the Lord has made known to us." So they went with haste and found Mary and Joseph, and the child lying in the manger. When they saw this, they made known what had been told them about this child; and all who heard it were amazed at what the shepherds told them. But Mary treasured all these words and pondered them in her heart. The shepherds returned, glorifying and praising God for all they had heard and seen, as it had been told them.

Good News!

Matthew 2:1-2

In the time of King Herod, after Jesus was born in Bethlehem of Judea, wise men from the East came to Jerusalem, asking, "Where is the child who has been born king of the Jews? For we observed his star at its rising, and have come to pay him homage."

Production and Presentation Notes

What Child Was This? brings together three complementary elements—music, drama, and worship—to create an exciting Christian education experience for children in grades 2 through 5.

Music, as a vehicle by which language and stories of faith are passed on, has few equals. Drama allows children to move beyond the limits of personal experience, exploring and expressing the thoughts and feelings of biblical figures, and learning more about their own thoughts and feelings.

The use of music and drama in worship reflects a growing appreciation for the educational function of congregational worship. Children involved in this musical receive a practical experience in leading worship. They discover that their presentation, rather than being a performance or entertainment, is a gift to the congregation—a retelling of the birth of Christ.

The Setting and Cast

What Child Was This? based on Luke 2:1-20 and Matthew 2:1-2, begins with a personal introduction; we meet Joseph as an older adult working in his carpentry shop. The story of Christ's birth unfolds as Joseph shares his memories of that special time. These memories come to life before our eyes as the cast enacts his telling of the story.

Mary and Young Joseph sing of their exhausting trip from Nazareth to Bethlehem. The shepherds tell us of their surprise and fear as angels sing on the hilltops. Kings from a foreign land travel to visit the child and are joined on the way by the shepherds and angels. Filled with excitement, the visitors speak louder and louder until the new father, Young Joseph, reminds them that the babe is sleeping. The group tiptoes away from the child and then joyfully sings "Born This Night" as it moves into the congregation.

One of the unique components of What Child Was This? is the flexibility in casting.

The musical ends with a beautiful reminder of the ultimate gift received through Christ's birth—the gift of salvation—as the congregation and cast sing the beloved carol, "What Child Is This." Composer John Horman has written an additional stanza to the hymn, reminding us that the Christ born many years ago is still present with us today.

One of the unique components of *What Child Was This?* is the flexibility in casting. The musical can be cast with as few or as many members as you wish. Determine the size of the cast based on whether the musical will be presented in worship or in another setting; the number of children involved (youth and adults may participate as well); and the amount of time needed for rehearsals. The primary characters are Mary (speaking and solo singing role), Young Joseph (speaking and solo singing role), and Old Joseph (speaking role). All other roles can be divided among children who wish to have a speaking and small group-singing role (Kings, Shepherds, and Angels); those who wish to play characters with no speaking but small group-singing parts (Servants); and those who wish to be primarily chorus members. Enable each child to feel comfortable and yet challenged in his or her role. To enhance the intergenerational possibilities of *What Child Was This?* invite adults and/or youth to portray some of the characters, such as Old Joseph.

Flexibility in casting also allows for a great deal of cooperation between the ministries of the church. The Sunday school and choir programs can produce this musical together by splitting responsibilities between a class, choir, or any combination that will work best for your situation. If the Sunday school traditionally produces the Christmas program, consider teaching the songs during Sunday school assembly time and have all the members of your Sunday school be the chorus.

The Sets, Props, and Costumes

What Child Was This? allows you to choose from a variety of options for setting the scene. You may want to consider the space in which you will be presenting the musical as well as the amount of time you have for preparation.

Create a stable scene using simple supplies, and place it in the center of the worship area. This placement will help the members of the congregation know that they, too, have come to visit Bethlehem. Choose three small areas in which to place the chorus, the Angels and Shepherds, and Joseph's workshop. (See page 36 for an illustration of the set.) Simple props, such as a bale of hay, one or two benches, and an unfinished manger help set the scene. Instructions for creating a life-size palm tree for the chorus area are included on page 38.

Working on the sets will get children, their families, and other members of the church community involved in the production of the musical. Several options are listed in "Get Set" on page 36. Meet with the persons who will be helping you with the production of *What Child Was This?* and decide which options best suit your setting and schedule.

Most of the cast will wear oversized T-shirts as the foundation of their costumes. After the T-shirts are dyed, cast members may decorate them according to their roles in the musical. Simple headdresses, belts, loose vests, and halos will complete the costumes of the Shepherds, Angels, Servants, and townspeople. Mary, Young Joseph, Old Joseph, and the Kings may wear adaptations of the basic costume or easy-to-make biblical costumes. Instructions for making costumes are included in "Costuming and Props" on page 39.

Preparation and Presentation

In addition to these production and presentation notes, *What Child Was This?* offers a step-by-step preparation and presentation process, providing leaders guidance for:

- exploring the characters of the story as real people with feelings much like our own
- learning the music
- learning pantomime and dramatic movement
- creating the sets and props
- developing costumes
- auditioning and rehearsing speaking roles and solos
- staging the musical
- preparing publicity materials
- helping the cast members understand their role as worship leaders

The plan for each session contains an overview of activities related to the session and detailed instructions for preparing the session—including a list of the materials needed. A section called "Into the Story" leads the teacher and students into learning the biblical content. "Into the Songs" guides the learning of the music. "Into the Drama" gives instructions for the group involved in production-related activities such as making the sets and props, preparing publicity, rehearsing specific roles, and so forth. In later sessions, "Into the Story" is replaced with "Into the Service," in which the participants focus on what it means to be a worship leader as the musical is presented. Each session also provides suggestions for a group closing time.

Schedules and Adaptations

Follow the suggested plan by scheduling sessions over the course of eight or nine weeks, with Session Nine (dress rehearsal) taking place the day before the presentation. Plan ninety-minute blocks of time for Sessions One through Eight, and a two-hour block for Session Nine—the dress rehearsal. Designating the presentation as Session Ten affirms the presentation as part of the total learning experience.

If church schedules cannot accommodate sessions of the suggested length, extend the preparation over additional weeks or eliminate some of the learning activities. Consider the time available, the number of children, the age range and musical abilities of the children, and adapt as your situation requires.

If you choose to condense the process into five longer sessions, combine Sessions One and Two, Sessions Three and Four, Sessions Five and Six, and Sessions Seven and Eight. Using this option, move from "Into the Story" and "Into the Songs" in the first of the combined sessions to the same categories in the second. Combine "Into the Drama" activities from both sessions, add a break/snack time,

What Child Was This? Components

Leader/Accompanist Edition

(Item Code No. 017912)

Contains production notes, script, music, and complete accompaniment; step-by-step session plans; and reproducible pages of instruction for set construction, auditions, staging, publicity, and costuming. An edition of this book is needed for persons leading the learning activities, teaching the music, and providing instrumental accompaniment.

Singer's Edition

(Item Code No. 017920)

Contains the biblical account, music (lyrics and melody line), narration and stage directions, learning activities, and an autograph page. One copy is needed for each singer and leader.

Listening Tape

(Item Code No. 017947)

Contains the complete musical with narration, songs, and full instrumentation. One copy is needed for the group.

Accompaniment Tape

(Item Code No. 017939)

Contains full instrumental accompaniment on Side A and full instrumental accompaniment with voices (singing only) in a split-track format on Side B.

and use closing devotions from the second session. Make similar adaptations for one-week choral camps and day camps.

Another possibility is to have a separate set and prop-creating workshop, and adapt the remainder of the sessions for use in your regular choir rehearsals. Consider holding a "Prepare for the Musical Day" when the children are out of school, such as on a teacher in-service day or on a Sunday afternoon. You could also create the sets after school, with parents providing snacks and transportation.

If your church has a small number of children, consider using *What Child Was This?* as an inter-generational experience. Adults and youth will find themselves captivated by the music, instruments, and dramatic story. Youth and adults will enjoy playing the flute, handbells/tone chimes, and percussion instruments. The children's natural musical abilities will be enhanced as they play the Orff-style accompaniment to "7b. Hush! Hush!" and add sleigh bells or camel bells to "6. Procession of the Kings."

Rehearsal Tactic

During the hectic period before Christmas, parents may be hesitant to commit themselves and their children to the *What Child Was This?* rehearsal schedule. Remind parents that the rehearsal time presents them with an opportunity to run errands and shop for Christmas gifts. Write a short letter to the parents encouraging them to:

STOP–stop at the church;
DROP–drop off their children for rehearsal;
SHOP–shop, shop, shop until rehearsal is over.

Leadership Needed

Leadership for *What Child Was This?* will be most effectively managed by two primary leaders. One leader will concentrate on learning activities related to the Bible lesson and music, and another leader will concentrate on the drama and production aspects of the musical. Recruit other leaders, helpers, and parents to:

• assist the children in creating the set (page 36)
• help coordinate auditions, line rehearsals, and staging (pages 42, 43, and 45)
• work as group leaders for Drama Centers and small groups in "Into the Drama" in Sessions One through Seven
• work with the children who are serving as Publicity Coordinators, Set Managers, and Costume Managers
• make or assign costumes and props (pages 39-41)

Enable all the children to feel ownership in the musical by letting them volunteer to be Publicity Coordinators, Stage Managers, and Costume Managers. See pages 36, 44, 45, and 39 for ideas on using the children in these roles.

Materials Needed

- ❏ Cassette player and *Listening Tape*
- ❏ *Singer's Editions*
- ❏ Name tag items
- ❏ Gold or yellow yarn
- ❏ Star stickers and gold stickers
- ❏ 3" x 5" or 4" x 6" index cards
- ❏ Index card file box
- ❏ Permanent markers, pencils, and crayons
- ❏ Laundry marker
- ❏ Materials for creating the set (see pages 36-38)
- ❏ Materials for "Costuming and Props" (see pages 39-41)
- ❏ Materials for "Preparing Publicity" (see page 44)
- ❏ Materials for "Staging the Story" (see page 45)
- ❏ Audition forms (see page 42)
- ❏ Posterboard, cardboard, and/or tagboard
- ❏ Paper or cloth bag
- ❏ Colored construction paper
- ❏ Hole punch
- ❏ No. 10 business envelopes
- ❏ Newsprint
- ❏ Masking tape and glue
- ❏ Drop cloths and painting shirts
- ❏ Music stands, chairs, and music scores
- ❏ Tempera paint
- ❏ Paintbrushes
- ❏ Butcher paper in various colors
- ❏ Scissors, stapler and staples
- ❏ Tables and chairs
- ❏ Ribbon
- ❏ Measuring tape, straight pins
- ❏ Hymnals
- ❏ Worship service bulletins
- ❏ 8 1/2" x 11" paper in various colors
- ❏ Dictionary, reference books
- ❏ Orff instruments (opt.)
- ❏ Camel/sleigh bells (opt.)
- ❏ Jump rope (opt.)
- ❏ Building blocks (opt.)
- ❏ Balloons (opt.)

Get Ready

Preparation of Materials

Planning Meeting

Meet with the other persons who will be sharing primary leadership. Review together the "Production and Presentation Notes," the "Into the Drama" sections, and the information in this section. Make decisions concerning the schedule, adaptations, and method of casting the musical. This meeting may also be a good time to review the materials needed and to confirm who will be responsible for enabling parents, youth, and other adults to participate in the production of *What Child Was This?* Decide how you will notify the children and others about the possibility of participation in the musical. Use a variety of publicity methods, such as your church newsletter, bulletin announcements, and posters to solicit opportunities for involvement.

A. Name Tags

Using the illustration shown, make a manger name tag for each child. Cut the name tag pattern from beige, ivory, or light brown paper. Cut out an additional "oval" from cardboard or posterboard for each tag. After the children have written their names on the name tags, help them to cut on the dotted line across the top of the manger. Using tape or glue, secure short pieces of gold yarn (hay) on the top back side of the manger and then push the yarn through the cut to the front. Glue the cardboard "oval" to the back of the manger to strengthen it. Punch holes as marked, and lace a piece of gold yarn through the holes to make a "neck-tag." (Using paper hole reinforcers will also strengthen the name tags.)

B. The Singers' Card File

The Singers' Card File will aid you in recording information about each child. Purchase 3" x 5" or 4" x 6" index cards and a file box in which to store the cards. Include the following on each child's card: name, address, age, grade, name of parent or guardian, and home telephone number. As the sessions progress, you may wish to add other information such as: hobbies, favorite school subjects, special concerns (for example, physical and social skill limitations, transportation problems, and so forth), and musical strengths and weaknesses. You could also note on the card if the singer's parent or guardian would like to assist the choir with production details. On the bottom of the card, record the child's attendance for each session.

NAME _____	AGE ____ GRADE ____	
ADDRESS _____	PHONE _____	
PARENT / GUARDIAN _____		
Hobbies _____		
Concerns _____		
Musical Info _____		

Session Attendance	1	2	3	4	5	6	7	8	9	10

C. Progress Bulletin Board

Using the map here as a reference, create a large map of Palestine in Jesus' time and staple it to a bulletin board. If no bulletin board is available, create a large mural out of butcher paper and tape it to a wall. Cut seven palm tree trunks out of brown construction paper using the pattern below. On each trunk write one of the song numbers and title. Staple the trunks in random places along the route from Nazareth to Bethlehem. Copy seven sets of the leaves on green construction paper and mark each as noted below. As you teach each song, the children will add palm leaves to the corresponding trunk to mark their progress. You will use several "Getting Better" leaves for each song.

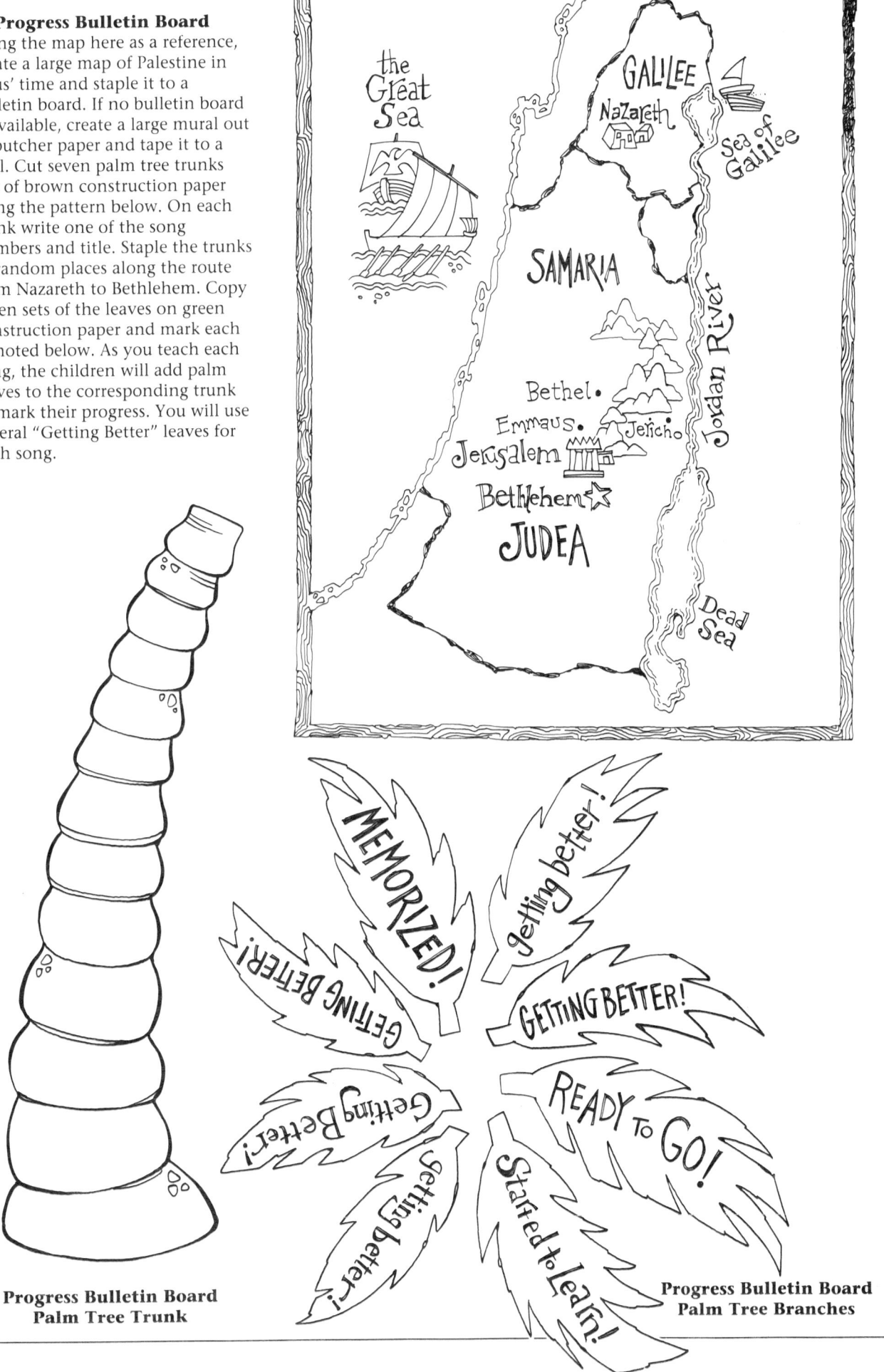

Progress Bulletin Board Palm Tree Trunk

Progress Bulletin Board Palm Tree Branches

D. N-S-E-W Bull's-Eye Chart

Using posterboard and permanent markers, create a chart using the picture here as a reference. Color the bull's-eye red, or use any color you think the children will enjoy.

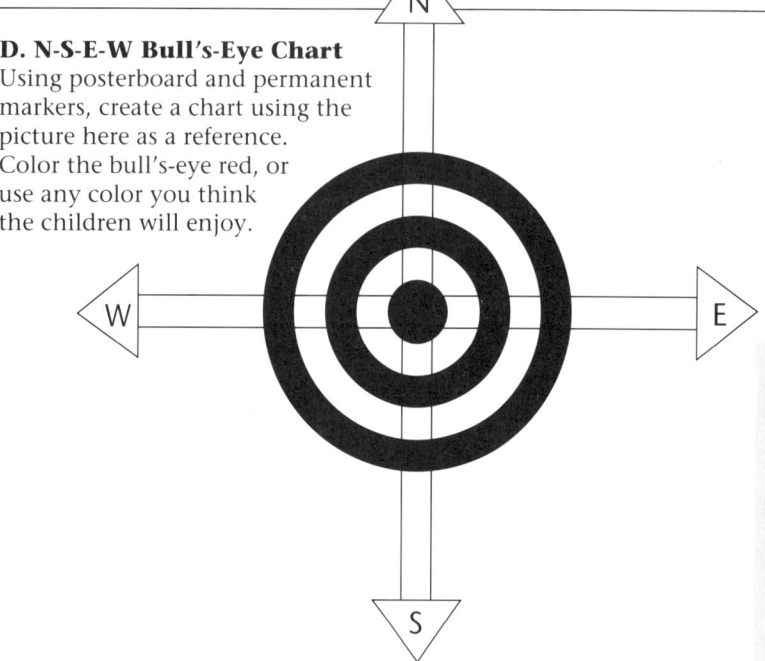

E. Consonant Squares

With 8 1/2" x 11" pieces of paper or posterboard and permanent markers, prepare a chart using the picture here as a reference. Write each consonant or consonant grouping on a separate piece of paper.

c	st	s	m
d	sh	t	n
ing	ce		

F. Warm-up Song

Beginning in Session Two, you will use a warm-up exercise as both a gathering song and a vocalise. Sing as notated below, and repeat as desired a half step higher or lower.

Glo - ry to God.   Glo - ry in the high   est.

G. Cast Announcement Poster

After the auditions in Session Three, create a "Cast Announcement Poster" using posterboard and permanent markers (or a computer). Place the poster in a visible location so the children will see it as they arrive. They will quickly discover who will play what role in the upcoming presentation. (Use the "Emperor Augustus' Registration Form" on page 20 of the *Singer's Edition* to help chorus members create names and roles for themselves.)

A N N O U N C I N G
What Child Was This?
by John Horman

Presented by: (name of group/choir, church)
Date:
Time:
Place:

CAST

ROLES	CHORUS
Old Joseph:	(Use Jewish children's names from "Emperor Augustus' Registration Form")
Mary:	
Young Joseph:	
Joseph:	
Angel 1:	David of Galilee:
Angel 2:	Martha of Bethlehem:
Shepherd 1:	
Shepherd 2:	
Shepherd 3:	
King 1:	
King 2:	
King 3:	
Servants:	

Stage Manager:
  Assistants:
Publicity Manager:
  Assistants:
Costume Manager:
  Assistants:

H. Creative Word Games

Use the following games as tools for learning the song texts. Emphasize the fun of playing, not winning.

• **Word Search.** Use the "Word Search" on page 18 of the *Singer's Edition* as a quiet activity.

• **Puzzle Activity.** Type or write the text of a song in large print on heavy tagboard. Cut the text into puzzle pieces, and place the pieces in a paper or cloth bag. Use the puzzle as an activity for an individual or a small group.

• **Noisy Mayhem Game.** Print the text of a song from the musical on a piece of paper, and cut the text into the same number of pieces as you have singers. (If you have a small group, choose one song for this game. Divide a large choir into two or more groups and use a different song for each group.) Pass a hat or bag with the pieces of paper in it, and ask each singer to pick one piece. When everyone has chosen a slip of paper, have the group stand. The children should stand in a line according to the order of the song text. Encourage them to sing their phrase over and over until they find their correct place in the line.

• **Jump Rope Rhymes.** Use the songs as jump rope rhymes, and see which child can jump the longest. Time the jumpers as they say or sing the text and jump.

• **Build a Tower.** To play this game, you will need a helper and building blocks. Ask the helper to read a portion of a song text, and have a child complete the sentence or phrase. If the child is correct, he or she may choose a block and construct a tower. See who can build the tallest tower.

• **Balloon Relay Race.** Gather several chairs, an inflated balloon for each child, and helpers. Place the chairs in a line several feet away from the children. Ask the children to face the chairs and stand one behind the other in two or more lines. Assign one helper to each line, and have the helpers simultaneously ask the children at the front of each line to complete a phrase of a song text. When a child answers correctly, he or she should receive a balloon, run to a chair, sit on and pop the balloon, and then run back to tag the next person in line.

• **Word Ball.** Set up an area in the shape of a softball field, with three bases and a home plate. Have the children form one line. The "batter" (the child at the front of the line) should supply the word in a phrase that the adult "pitches" to him or her. The batter may move from one base to the next with each correct answer. Three "strikes" means the batter must move to the back of the line to try again.

• **Word Relay.** Write the words from a refrain on posterboard, and cut apart by individual words or phrases. (See example below.) Have the children form two or more lines. Give the person at the head of each line a piece of board, and have him or her place it face-up on the floor. As teammates move to the front of the line, they too will receive pieces of the board until all pieces are distributed. Team members should place their pieces of text in the correct order on the floor. See which team can complete the refrain the fastest.

| ALL | THEY | WANT | ARE | TAXES |

I. "All the Sky Was Filled with Angels" Crossword Puzzle

The answers to the crossword puzzle found on pages 22-23 of the *Singer's Edition* are listed here for your convenience.

ACROSS
1. As they _____ for generations
3. Of peace and _____
4. _____ huddled in the cold
7. Tidings of great joy _____ bring
8. All the sky was _____ed
9. Lifting heart and _____
11. _____, glory in the highest
14. Burst forth _____ singing
15. Angel _____ swept
16. Burst forth with _____

DOWN
2. And the night gave up its _____
5. Swept 'cross the _____
6. _____ heart and soul and head
10. Singing of a newborn _____
12. Great joy we _____
13. That the _____ had foretold
15. All the sky _____ filled with angels
17. Then the _____ burst

¹H	A	²D				³J	O	Y
		R		⁵H				
⁴S	H	E	P	H	E	R	D	¹⁷S
		A		A				K
		D		V				Y
⁶L			⁷W	E				
I				N				
⁸F	I	L	L		⁹S	O	U	L
T								
I			¹⁰B				¹³P	
N		¹²B	O				R	
¹¹G	L	O	R	Y			O	
			I				P	
			N		¹⁴W	I	T	H
¹⁵W	I	N	G	S			E	
A							T	
¹⁶S	I	N	G	I	N	G	S	

9

Session One

Preparation

Materials
- [ ] Cassette player and *Listening Tape*
- [ ] *Singer's Editions*
- [ ] The Singers' Card File
- [ ] Star stickers
- [ ] Name tags
- [ ] Glue
- [ ] Pieces of yellow or gold yarn
- [ ] One long piece of yellow or gold yarn for each child
- [ ] Cardboard ovals for name tags
- [ ] Hole punch
- [ ] Masking tape
- [ ] Newsprint/large sheet of paper and a dictionary
- [ ] Permanent markers and crayons
- [ ] Paper, ribbon, and gold sticker for "Decree from Augustus"
- [ ] T-shirts and dye for adult leader T-shirts
- [ ] Pencils
- [ ] Progress Bulletin Board materials
- [ ] Notes to parents

Set Up the Rehearsal Area
The basic set-up of the rehearsal area will be the same for each session. In one section of the room, arrange the chairs in a circle or standard choir formation. Leave an open space where the children can sit on the floor and/or play action games. If space allows, provide one or more tables with chairs. Put the cassette recorder in a central location so that the *Listening Tape* can be heard throughout the room.

Create the Progress Bulletin Board
See the instructions on page 7 for preparing the Progress Bulletin Board.

Prepare to Use Attendance Charts
Prepare to use the *What Child Was This?* Attendance Chart found on page 19 in the *Singer's Edition*. Gather star attendance stickers. The children will place stickers on the chart for each session they attend.

Prepare Name Tags
See page 6 for instructions. Ask a helper to prepare the manger name tags for you.

Write and Make Copies of Note for Parents
Prepare a note to the parents reminding them that each child will need a white T-shirt for the next session. Include the rehearsal schedule and suggest ways parents can be volunteer helpers. List your phone number, and invite them to call you to volunteer their assistance.

Create a "Decree from Augustus"
On a piece of paper write the following in large letters: "I, Emperor Augustus, hereby decree that all persons should return to their places of birth to be registered. I also decree that each person should be taxed." Roll up the "decree," seal it with a gold sticker, and tie it with a bright ribbon.

Prepare T-shirts for the Adult Leaders
Dye the T-shirts for the leaders, and remind them to wear the shirts to the first rehearsal. (See page 40 of "Costuming and Props" for information about dyeing the T-shirts.)

Review Session Plans
Review the session plans so one section will easily flow into the next.

Into the Story

Welcome the Children
Play the recording of *What Child Was This?* as you welcome the children. Ask each child to write his or her name on a manger name tag in large letters and then glue the yarn hay into place. Let a helper assist the children in gluing the oval on the back of the tags, punching two holes in the tags, and lacing the long piece of yarn through the holes. Update the Singers' Card File.

Gathering Activity
Children who have completed their name tags may begin coloring their Attendance Charts (*Singer's Edition*, page 19). An older youth helper can encourage the children in this activity.

Introduce the Story: Luke
Distribute pencils and copies of the *Singer's Edition*, and have the children write their names on the back covers. Ask the children to turn to page 1 and follow along as you read the story from Luke 2:1-20. Consider asking an older child who is a strong reader, or a youth to read this passage. Ask the children if they find any unfamiliar words. Write these words on a large piece of paper or newsprint. Let the children share definitions, and have a dictionary handy to use as a reference. Write the definitions on newsprint, and then re-read the sentence in which the word(s) appear.

Live the Story: Trip from Nazareth
Ask the children to sit in a circle on the floor, and join them in the circle. Read to them the "Decree of Emperor Augustus." Tell them where you were born, and discuss how long it would take to travel there. Ask the children, "Where were you born?" "How would you travel there? By car, train, plane?" "What would you take with you on the trip?"

Show them the map of Palestine on the Progress Bulletin Board, and trace with your finger the route from Nazareth to Bethlehem. To help them understand the distance, mention a city or place that is between sixty to seventy miles from your church. Tell the children that Joseph and Mary traveled by walking or riding on a donkey. They took only those things that were necessary for survival such as food, water, and a mantle or cloak to sleep on. Remind them that the trip was dangerous because robbers knew that travelers were carrying money to pay their taxes.

Into the Songs

Introduce "2. Taxes, Taxes"
Tell the children that the first song they are going to learn sets the scene of the musical. Many of the people in Bethlehem were tired because they had traveled a long way, and they had to make the trip to pay taxes. This song deals with paying taxes, Caesar Augustus' decree, and Mary and Joseph's long journey.

Have the children turn to page 3 in the *Singer's Edition* to find "2. Taxes, Taxes." Ask them to put their opened books on the floor in front of them, and lead them in tapping the pulse of the song on their thighs. As they tap, explain that "2. Taxes, Taxes" is a speech chorus. Then begin speaking the refrain of the song. Repeat the chant, encouraging the children to join you.

When the children are comfortable speaking the chant, begin lightly tapping on the floor next to your music and say the first stanza. Ask them to follow along, tapping on their music as you say stanza 1. Have the children join you when you begin the refrain. To add interest, periodically change the way you tap the beat. Try snapping the beat with your fingers, tapping the floor, alternate hands tapping, and so forth.

Ask the children if they have heard the text of stanza 1 before. (Yes, from the Bible story.) Have them say stanza 1 with you and then stand. Move in a circle, stepping on the beat while everyone says the refrain, stanza 1, and the refrain together. As the children finish the refrain following stanza 1, continue tapping the beat. Speaking in rhythm, ask the children to pick up their music and walk in time to their chairs. Continue tapping the beat until every child has found a seat. (Remember to change the way you tap the beat to add interest.)

Introduce "3. We've Come So Far"
Tell them to open their *Singer's Editions* to page 5 to find "3. We've Come So Far." Explain to them that Mary, Joseph, and the chorus will tell the story of the trip from Nazareth to Bethlehem through this song. Tell them they are going to listen to the song in a special way. They should raise a hand when they hear a soloist sing, raise both hands when they hear two soloists singing together (a duet), and stand when they hear the chorus sing. (You will need to do the movements with them to help the younger singers.)

Play the recording of "3. We've Come So Far." After listening to the song, ask the children to help you find the page and measure number where the chorus first sings in the song (page 6, letter C, measure 30). Speak the chorus text together. Play or sing the melody of this section and ask the children to follow along, silently mouthing the text. Then let the children stand and sing this section.

Compliment them, and have them form a circle near the Progress Bulletin Board. Encourage the children to echo-sing whatever you sing. (They will not need to look at their books.) Begin by singing measures 60-61, "On their way." Motion for the children to sing this back to you. Repeat these measures again and have them echo. If they are having difficulty with a specific interval, point to your ear to remind them to listen. Then sing the problem interval slowly. Once the children are secure in the singing of this phrase, sing the final phrase of the song (measures 62-65), and have them echo.

Progress Bulletin Board and Review

Show the children the Progress Bulletin Board. Explain that as they achieve a level of success, one of them will get to add a branch to the palm tree for that song. Tell the children that "Started to Learn" means the first time they have worked on the music; "Getting Better" means that there is definite progress; "Memorized" means they can sing the song without music; and "Ready to Go!" means that the song (including motions and/or staging) is performance-ready!

Ask the children to stand and chant the refrain and first stanza of "2. Taxes, Taxes." Then have them sing the chorus parts of "3. We've Come So Far." (They may use their books.) Choose a child to tape a "Started to Learn" branch on the "2. Taxes, Taxes," and "3. We've Come So Far" tree trunks. (Attach the leaves to the trunks with a loop of masking tape placed on the back of the leaves.)

Into the Drama

Discuss Auditions
Share with the children that auditions will be held during the third session. All children should audition, even if they are not interested in a solo part, so you can determine what they would like to do in the musical. Tell them that most of the time the acting in *What Child Was This?* will be pantomimed.

Play "Simon Says" Game
To help the children explore the various responses of the chorus in the musical, play "Simon Says" with them. Use statements such as "Simon says look surprised"; "Simon says look sad"; "Simon says wave to a baby"; "Simon says shake your head no"; "Simon says act afraid."

Explain Costuming
Tell the children that everyone will wear a costume in the presentation.

Share with them how the chorus will be dressed. Remind the children that Augustus commanded everyone—persons of all ages, poor and wealthy alike—to return to the cities of their birth. Ask the children to begin thinking about what character they would like to play. Would the character be old or young, rich or poor? How did the character earn money? For example, was he or she a farmer, shepherd, merchant, or innkeeper?

Closing

Bring the Children Together
Ask all of the helpers, children, and parents to join you in the closing. Thank the children for coming and congratulate them on the work they have done. Remind them that it is important to attend all the rehearsals. Tell them that each week as they arrive, there will be a variety of things to do. They may play a game or they may want to finish coloring a worksheet. Tell them that you will sing a warm-up song when it is time to begin rehearsal. When they hear the song, they are to finish what they are doing and move to their chairs. Sing the warm-up song (see page 8) for them and ask them to join you in singing it. Ask them to bring their T-shirts to the next rehearsal.

Pray Together
Have the children bow their heads and close their eyes while you play the recording of "9b. What Child Is This." They may join in singing the refrain if they already know it. At the close of the song, lead the children in the prayer below:

> *We thank you, God, for sending Jesus. Help us to be joyful as we share with others the excitement of the birth of your Son. Amen.*

Name Tags, Attendance Charts, and Notes
As you collect the name tags, personally thank each child by name for coming. Ask a youth or adult helper to help the children place star stickers on their Attendance Charts, collect the *Singer's Editions*, and give them a copy of the T-shirt reminder letter.

Review
Meet with the primary leaders and review what needs to be done for the next rehearsal. Evaluate Session One and make adaptations to the next session as needed. Remind them to wear their T-shirts again next week.

Session Two

Preparation

Materials
- ❏ Cassette player and *Listening Tape*
- ❏ *Singer's Editions*
- ❏ The Singers' Card File
- ❏ Star stickers
- ❏ Name tags
- ❏ Masking tape
- ❏ Materials for N-S-E-W Bull's-Eye Chart
- ❏ Permanent markers and crayons
- ❏ Pencils
- ❏ Reference books
- ❏ Laundry marker
- ❏ Progress Bulletin Board materials

Make the N-S-E-W Bull's-Eye Chart
Using the instructions and illustration on page 8, prepare the N-S-E-W Bull's-Eye Chart.

Prepare to Use "What a Charcter You Are!" and the "Emperor Augustus' Registration Form"
These forms are found on pages 20-21 of the *Singer's Edition*. Be ready to help the children complete the forms. Make sure you have a pencil for each child and reference books available.

Review Session Plans
Review the plans for this session to ensure a smooth flow throughout the rehearsal.

Into the Story

Welcome the Children
Play the recording of *What Child Was This?* as you welcome the children. Write each child's name in the back of his or her costume T-shirt with a laundry marker. Ask helpers to assist new children in creating manger name tags. Update the Singers' Card File.

Gathering Activities
Children who have completed their name tags may begin or continue coloring their Attendance Charts (*Singer's Edition*, page 19). An older youth helper can encourage the children in this. Ask a helper to play the drama game "Simon Says" with the children. Then have another helper lead the speech chant "2. Taxes, Taxes." (If desired, you may form two groups and do these two activities simultaneously.)

Warm Up Voices
As you begin to sing the warm-up on page 8, encourage the children to move to their rehearsal places. Model clear, pure vowel sounds and consonants for the children. Have them sing the warm-up with you.

Into the Story: Angels and Shepherds
Tell the children that you will read a passage of scripture about angels and shepherds. Ask the children to listen for two key words—*angels* and *shepherds*. Each time you say the word *shepherd*, they are to put a hand above their eyes as though they were looking for a lost sheep. When you say the word *angel*, they should hook their thumbs together and wiggle their fingers as though their hands were angel wings. Read Luke 2:8-20 from page 1 of this book.

Live the Story: Key Elements
Ask the children to pretend that they are the shepherds in the biblical story. Can they tell their story to you? Listen for the correct order of events according to Luke's Gospel: shepherds are watching their flocks in the field; an angel appears and tells them Christ has been born in Bethlehem; suddenly a whole multitude of angels appears singing "Glory to God"; the angels leave, and the shepherds decide to go to Bethlehem; the shepherds find Mary, Joseph, and the baby and tell them about the visit of the angels; everyone is amazed, and the shepherds return to their flocks, praising God.

Into the Songs

Introduce "4. All the Sky Was Filled with Angels"
Distribute copies of the *Singer's Edition*, and have the children turn to "4. All the Sky Was Filled with Angels" (page 8). Share with them that the Angels, Shepherds, and the chorus convey part of Luke's message through this song. The chorus sets the scene; the Shepherds and Angels each tell their story; and then the chorus sings the Shepherds' and the Angels' songs together.

Play the tune to stanza 1 on the piano as the children listen. Ask them to put their music on their laps. They should tap their shoulders lightly on the beat as you play the melody of stanza 1 again. Have the children stand, holding their music, and say with you the text of stanza 1 in rhythm. Repeat this stanza, singing the text.

Ask the children whose first names begin with the letters A through J to sing the stanza for you. Listen for those who are having difficulty matching pitch or singing the text. Make a mental note of

these children so you can work with them in small groups during next week's "Gathering" time. Let the children whose first names begin with letters K through Z sing stanza 1. Note again the children with whom you will need to spend a little extra time.

Ask the children to read together the text of stanza 2. Tell them to move into a circle, bringing their books with them. Play the melody of stanza 2 as the children move around in a circle in time to the music. Have them sit and echo-sing each phrase after you. Correct problem spots by singing the intervals slowly and having the children echo. Make a game out of this activity by pretending that you are a mime. Use only hand motions to instruct the children when to sing and when to listen—don't speak at all during this section of the rehearsal.

Review "2. Taxes, Taxes"
Begin to chant the refrain of "2. Taxes, Taxes." How many of the children remember the text from

the last rehearsal? Teach the text of stanza 1 a sentence at a time. Make a game out of the learning process by asking one child to listen to the group's diction. The child should give the group a 1 to 10 grade based on how clearly the group says the text (10 is the highest grade, and 1 the lowest). Remind the child to listen for clear consonants and for good unison speech.

Ask the children to open their books to page 4 and find stanza 2. Begin tapping the beat, and then let them read the text together. Speak the text two times as the children listen and tap. When you read stanza 2 the first time, speak it on one pitch with no inflection. As you say the text again, add inflection, raising and lowering the pitch of your speaking voice as the meaning of the text dictates. Ask the children to tell you the difference between the two versions of stanza 2. How did you speak it? (All on one pitch versus speaking with a rise and fall to your voice.) Ask the children to say the whole speech chorus for you with inflection. Make a mental note of places in the text that you will need to review next week.

Review "3. We've Come So Far"
Review the chorus parts of "3. We've Come So Far," reminding the children that Joseph and Mary tell some of the story through solos and a duet. Show the children the N-S-E-W Bull's-Eye Chart, and ask them to make a "north-south mouth" (vertical mouth opening). Ask them to sing the letter C section again on "ah" using a "north-south mouth." Then have the children sing the text. Hold up the chart, and trace the N-S axis with your finger as they sing measures 33-34 ("two; search for"), and measures 41-42 ("wide welcome them"). Also use the N-S-E-W Bull's-Eye Chart for the text, "on their way" (measures 60-61, 62-63).

Progress Bulletin Board
Add the "Getting Better" leaf to the "2. Taxes, Taxes" and "3. We've Come So Far" palm trees. Add the "Started to Learn" leaf to the "4. All the Sky Was Filled with Angels" palm tree.

Into the Drama

Auditions Reminder
Tell the children that next week they will be singing and reading for you. Even if they aren't interested in a solo part, they should audition so you can find out what they are interested in doing. Share with them the possibility of being a Costume Manager, Stage Manager, Publicity Coordinator, and so forth.

Fill Out "What a Character You Are!" and the "Emperor Augustus' Registration Form"
Hand out pencils, and have the children turn to pages 20-21 in their books. Work with the children in filling out the two pages, completing page 21 first. Older youth and parents can assist small groups of children in deciding who they would like to be in the musical. Let the adult working with costumes see the completed forms. Use the map on the Progress Bulletin Board as a resource for potential "birth places." Have reference books handy that contain biblical names, possible occupations, and so forth. Check with your pastor for additional resources.

Learn Song Movements
Begin to work on the chorus movements for "3. We've Come So Far" and the movements to stanzas 1 and 2 of "4. All the Sky Was Filled with Angels." (See "Get Moving," pages 46-47). Say the text in rhythm as the children do the movements. Link the movements to specific words as much as possible. Play a few rounds of "Simon Says" using specifics from the script: for example, "Simon says you are shepherds scared by the sudden appearance of angels"; "Simon says you are the innkeepers saying 'no' to Mary and Joseph"; "Simon says you are a member of a crowd holding signs against taxation."

Closing

Bring the Children Together
Move into a circle and thank the children for their work during this rehearsal. Remind them that every rehearsal is important. Review with them what they have accomplished so far. They have:
- worked on "2. Taxes, Taxes"
- worked on chorus parts and movement of "3. We've Come So Far"
- worked on stanzas 1 and 2 and movement of "4. All the Sky Was Filled with Angels"
- decided on characters for themselves
- worked on actions for some of the situations in the musical

Pray Together
Remind the children of Luke 2:20: "The shepherds returned, glorifying and praising God for all they had heard and seen, as it had been told them." Pray the prayer below.

Dear God, help us to live our lives filled with praise for you. Give us hearts filled with joy so that we, like the shepherds, will return to our homes and schools rejoicing in your love. We pray this in the name of Jesus Christ, our Lord. Amen.

Name Tags, Attendance Charts, and Notes
As you collect the name tags, personally thank each child by name for coming. Ask a youth or adult helper to help the children place star stickers on the Attendance Charts and collect the *Singer's Editions*. Give any new children a copy of the T-shirt reminder letter.

Review
Meet with the primary leaders and review what needs to be done for the next rehearsal. Review the "Emperor Augustus' Registration Forms," compiling a list of specific needs for costumes. Adapt plans for the next session as needed.

Session Three

Preparation

Materials
❑ Cassette player and *Listening Tape*
❑ *Singer's Editions*
❑ The Singers' Card File
❑ Star stickers
❑ Name tags
❑ Masking tape
❑ Supplies for Drama Centers
❑ Permanent markers and crayons
❑ Newsprint or a large piece of paper
❑ Dictionary
❑ Pencils
❑ N-S-E-W Bull's-Eye Chart
❑ Audition forms
❑ Costume supplies, dye, T-shirts
❑ Laundry marker
❑ Progress Bulletin Board materials

Dye the Children's T-shirts
Dye the children's T-shirts according to the information they wrote on the "Emperor Augustus' Registration Forms" on page 20 of their *Singer's Editions*. (See page 40 of "Costuming and Props" for information about dyeing the T-shirts.)

Arrange for Drama Center and Audition Rooms
Arrange for a room in which to create Drama Centers. If you have a large group of children, you may need more than one area. Place supplies for each center (such as headdress, palm tree, and tax sign materials) on a separate table. Arrange to have another room that will provide privacy for auditions.

Get Drama Helpers
Have plenty of helpers so the primary drama leader can "float" between centers. Let the helpers facilitate moving the groups between centers.

Prepare Supplies for Costumes
Have all supplies for the costumes prepared. (See "Costuming and Props," page 39.)

Prepare Supplies for "TAXES" Signs
Have all supplies for the "TAXES" signs prepared. (See "Costuming and Props," page 41.)

Prepare Supplies for Palm Tree
Gather the supplies for the palm tree. (See "Get Set," page 38.)

Copy the Audition Form
Make one copy of the audition form for each child. (See "Holding Auditions," page 42.) Write in the child's name, age, and gender in advance.

Prepare to Use the "All the Sky Was Filled with Angels" Puzzle
Review the crossword puzzle on pages 22-23 of the *Singer's Edition*. Note that the answers to the puzzle are printed on page 9 of this guide.

Review Session Plans
Study the plans for this session, and mentally divide the children into groups.

Into the Story

Welcome the Children
Play the recording of *What Child Was This?* as you welcome the children. Write the names in the back of any costume T-shirts that are brought in this week. Encourage the children to find a group and participate in one of the following activities. Update the Singers' Card File.

Gathering Activities
Children who haven't finished coloring their Attendance Charts should complete them. An older youth helper can encourage the children in this. Ask three helpers to space themselves around the room and encourage the children to play the drama game "Simon Says"; to review the movements of "3. We've Come So Far" and "4. All the Sky Was Filled with Angels"; and to practice the speech chorus, "2. Taxes, Taxes." Work with the children who had difficulty matching pitch or singing the text last week.

Warm Up Voices
Encourage the children to move to their rehearsal places as they sing the warm-up on page 8. Model clear vowel sounds and consonants for the children.

Into the Story: "What Child Is This"
Ask the children to open their *Singer's Editions* to "9b. What Child Is This" (page 17). Read the text of the hymn together. Are there any unfamiliar words? If so, write these on a piece of large paper or newsprint. Give the children an opportunity to share a definition, and have a dictionary handy to use as a reference. Write the definition on the newsprint. Then read the sentence in which the word(s) appear one more time.

Live the Story: Composer/Author
Sing together the refrain of "9b. What Child Is This" (*Singer's Edition*, page 17). Tell the children that the tune of this song is called GREENSLEEVES. Help them find the tune name on the page. Mention that the tune is a sixteenth-century English melody, and help them find this credit. Ask, "Who wrote the words, and where are their names on the page?" (Stanzas 1, 2, and 3 were written by William Dix in 1865, and John Horman has written stanza 4.) Remind the singers of the characters in Luke's Gospel, and help them find these characters in the text of "What Child Is This." (Mary, shepherds, angels.)

Into the Songs

Introduce Stanzas 3 and 4 of "4. All the Sky Was Filled with Angels"
Have the children locate stanzas 3 and 4 in the *Singer's Edition* (stanza 3: page 8, letter A; stanza 4: page 8, letter B). Ask them to turn to the section where the melodies of these two stanzas are sung together (page 9, letter C). Sing together the Angels' song, which begins at letter C. Tell the children to follow the Angels' words (Part I) with their fingers as they sing this section. Then ask them to sing the Shepherds' song, which begins at letter C. Follow the same procedure as above. Ask the children to sing Part I while the melody of Part II is played on the piano; then have the children sing Part II as Part I is played on the piano. Challenge them to sing the parts together. Divide into two groups and try to sing both parts simultaneously. Assign the older youth and adult helpers to a group, and have them sing with that particular group.

After singing, help the children complete the "All the Sky Was Filled with Angels" crossword puzzle on pages 22-23 of the *Singer's Edition*.

Review "2. Taxes, Taxes"
Find "2. Taxes, Taxes" in the *Singer's Edition* (page 3). Review and begin working on memorization.

Review "3. We've Come So Far"
Review the chorus parts of "3. We've Come So Far" (pages 6, 7). Add the movements as listed on page 46 of this book. Using the N-S-E-W Bull's-Eye Chart, visually remind the children to open their mouths and drop their jaws.

Progress Bulletin Board
Add "Getting Better" leaves as appropriate.

Into the Drama

Audition and Drama Centers
Ask the children to sit with you in a circle. Tell them that they will begin working on costumes, "TAXES" signs, and the palm tree this rehearsal and the next. Explain that a helper will come to get them when it is time for their auditions.

Divide the children into three groups, and rotate them among the following work centers.
- Center 1: Headdress- and girdle-making center
- Center 2: Palm tree-making center
- Center 3: "TAXES" sign-making center

Have a helper bring the children one by one to the audition area. Ask and expect the children to clean up the Drama Centers as they complete a project. Use masking tape to mark each child's headdress, girdle, and sign.

Closing

Bring the Children Together
Compliment them for working together in groups, and thank them for meeting with you in the auditions. Mention that you will post the audition results on the door prior to the next rehearsal. Ask them to open their *Singer's Editions* to "9b. What Child Is This" (page 17) and sing together stanza 1.

Pray Together
Ask the children to join you in the following prayer, repeating each phrase after you.

> *Dear God, we thank you for sending us Christ the King. Help us to remember why we celebrate Christmas, and help us always to sing your praises. Glory in the highest! Help us bring tidings of great joy to our friends and families. Amen.*

Name Tags and Attendance Charts
As you collect the name tags, personally thank each child by name for auditioning. Ask a helper to help the children place star stickers on the Attendance Charts and collect the *Singer's Editions*.

Review
Meet with the primary leaders, and review what needs to be done for the next rehearsal. Review the success of the Drama Centers, and adjust plans as needed. Make adaptations to the plans for the next session as needed. Review possible role assignments with the Drama Leader, and finalize the cast. In addition to the main characters, use the "Emperor Augustus' Registration Form" to assign every child in the chorus a name and role. (See *Singer's Editions*, page 20.)

Notes

Session Four

OVERVIEW

Preparation
Create Cast Announcement Poster
Address Envelopes
Arrange to Meet with Instrumentalists
Arrange for Drama Center Helpers
Arrange for Rehearsal Areas
Gather Orff Instruments
Review Session Plans

Into the Story
Welcome the Children
Gathering Activities
Warm Up Voices
Into the Story: Names of Jesus
Live the Story: Creative Art

Into the Songs
Introduce "5. Born This Night"
Review "4. All the Sky Was Filled with Angels"
Review "2. Taxes, Taxes"
Listen to "3. We've Come So Far"
Progress Bulletin Board

Into the Drama
Scene Groups and Drama Centers

Closing
Bring the Children Together
Pray Together
Name Tags and Attendance Charts
Review

Preparation

Materials
- ❏ Cassette player and *Listening Tape*
- ❏ *Singer's Editions*
- ❏ The Singers' Card File
- ❏ Star stickers
- ❏ Name tags
- ❏ No. 10 business envelopes
- ❏ Supplies for Drama Centers
- ❏ Permanent markers and crayons
- ❏ Paper
- ❏ Orff instruments
- ❏ Pencils
- ❏ N-S-E-W Bull's-Eye Chart
- ❏ Cast Announcement Poster
- ❏ Progress Bulletin Board materials

Create Cast Announcement Poster
Using the illustration on page 8, prepare the Cast Announcement Poster. Complete the form and post it on the door of the rehearsal room.

Address Envelopes
Address envelopes to the homebound, persons in the hospital, and so forth. The children will compose prayers during the "Live the Story" section of this session. These prayers will be mailed to persons in need.

Arrange to Meet with Instrumentalists
Contact the instrumentalists, and schedule a separate rehearsal with them.

Arrange for Drama Center Helpers
Have plenty of helpers to assist in the Drama Centers.

Arrange for Rehearsal Areas
Secure rehearsal rooms for the Drama Leader and the primary cast members.

Gather Orff Instruments
If your church does not have Orff instruments, contact a local school or church and ask if you could borrow their instruments. Be prepared to practice the Orff accompaniment to "7b. Hush! Hush!" during the "Gathering" time. Review the accompaniment, and decide in advance who will play which part.

Review Session Plans
Study the plans for this session, and work toward maintaining a smooth flow from one activity to the next.

19

Into the Story

Welcome the Children
Play the recording of "5. Born This Night" as you welcome the children. Encourage the children to find a group and participate in an activity. Work with Young Joseph and Mary on their solos in "3. We've Come So Far." Enlist other helpers to meet with Old Joseph to read through his lines. Update the Singers' Card File.

Gathering Activities
Assign each helper a specific activity. Have the helpers space themselves around the room and encourage the children to work on word games (see "Get Ready," page 9); to play "Simon Says"; to review the movements of "3. We've Come So Far" and "4. All the Sky Was Filled with Angels"; and to work on memorizing "2. Taxes, Taxes" and "4. All the Sky Was Filled with Angels." Begin working with the children who will be playing the Orff instruments in "7b. Hush! Hush!"

Warm Up Voices
As the children move to their rehearsal places, lead them in singing the warm-up on page 8. Model clear vowel sounds and consonants for the children. Begin using phrases of the songs that need special attention as warm-ups.

Into the Story: Names of Jesus
Read Luke 2:10 to the children. Ask, "What was the good news the angel brought to the shepherds?" (Jesus is born.) Read the verse again and ask, "What were the names the angel called Jesus?" (Savior, Messiah, the Lord.) Tell them that Mary and Joseph named the baby "Jesus" because an angel told them to do so. "Jesus" means "Jehovah's salvation." Look for other names for Jesus that are in the script (see *Singer's Edition*). Some examples are: Angel 2 calls Jesus "Christ, the Lord" (page 7); the Kings call him "King of the Jews" (page 11); Mary calls him the "Prince of Peace" (page 16), and Young Joseph calls Jesus "Emmanuel, God with us" (page 16).

Live the Story: Creative Art
Ask the children to write a prayer or draw a picture using one or more of the names of Jesus. Tell them that these prayers and pictures will be sent to persons who need a special touch at this time—the homebound, persons in the hospital, those in need. Use the pre-addressed envelopes.

Into the Songs

Introduce "5. Born This Night"
In an excited stage whisper, speak the text of measures 6-17 (letter A) in rhythm several times. Motion for the children to join you in their whisper voices. Once the children are comfortable saying the text, have the pianist play the accompaniment of measures 1-17 while you and the children move in a circle. Step in time as you whisper the text. Step and whisper the text once more while the pianist plays the melody line. Ask the children to stand still and sing measures 6-17. Listen for the same excitement in their voices that you heard when they were whispering and moving.

Correct any wrong notes, and then sing the A section in a variety of ways. First, have the group sing the melody *staccato* (very short); then sing it *legato* (very smooth). Can the children combine the two styles of singing—smooth but with excitement and accent? Encourage them to enunciate clearly. Listen to the way they sing the word *us*. Be sure that the vowel sound is sustained and the "s" sound is short.

Review "4. All the Sky Was Filled with Angels"
Creating two small circles, divide the children into Part I (Angels) and Part II (Shepherds) according to the casting and the chorus. Help the children find their parts in the music using text, measure numbers, and rehearsal letters. Sing the entire song through several times, stopping to fix problem spots. To help the children sing section C in two parts, you may have the pianist play one part while you sing the other, or ask several helpers to sing with a specific part.

Review "2. Taxes, Taxes"
Ask the children to stand in small groups around you and speak the text, adding facial expressions and some motions of their own. Correct any problem spots, listen for clear enunciation, and work toward a good choral speech sound. Remind the children that they are to speak, rather than yell, the text. Have them stand together in a large group, and then move as far away from them as possible. Holding the N-S-E-W Bull's-Eye Chart, encourage the children to project their voices to the bull's-eye without losing a clear tone.

Listen to "3. We've Come So Far"
Have the children return to their seats and locate "3. We've Come So Far" in their books (page 5). As they listen to the recording of this song, they should follow along in their music. Sing the song in its entirety, helping Mary and Joseph as needed, so the children can see how these two characters fit into the piece.

Progress Bulletin Board
Add leaves to the palm trees as appropriate. The trees for "2. Taxes, Taxes," "3. We've Come So Far," "4. All the Sky Was Filled with Angels," and "5. Born This Night" should have some leaves. Add leaves for the instrumental songs ("1. Overture," "6. Procession of the Kings," and "9b. What Child Is This") as appropriate.

Into the Drama

Scene Groups and Drama Centers

While the Drama Leader and helpers work with one scene-grouping at a time (Kings and Servants; Shepherds 1, 2, and 3 and Angels 1 and 2; Young Joseph, Old Joseph, and Mary), other children may work in the Drama Centers. Enable the children to complete their costumes and "TAXES" signs during this session. As needed, have a helper assist the children with word games (see "Get Ready," page 9) and the prayers/pictures from "Live the Story." The Drama Leader should lead the main characters in reading their lines and blocking the scene-groupings.

Closing

Bring the Children Together

Thank the children for working hard to memorize the song texts and script. Arrange to meet with some of the main characters for brief, special rehearsals before or after each session. During these rehearsals, you will help them learn their solos and speaking lines. Schedule Young Joseph for a short rehearsal during the "Welcoming" time in the upcoming session. The Stage Managers, Costume Managers, and so forth will have a planning meeting with their adult helpers during the next session. Answer any questions the children may have. Review quickly what they have accomplished, and thank them for their hard work.

Pray Together

Listen to the recording of "9b. What Child Is This," singing the stanzas and refrain as the children are able. Then pray the prayer below.

> *Almighty God, we thank you for your gift of Emmanuel, God with us. We know that you are with us, just as you were with Mary, Joseph, the shepherds, the kings, and the servants. Use us, Lord, to spread the Good News of your Son, the Prince of Peace, Jesus the Christ, our Savior. Amen.*

Name Tags and Attendance Charts

Collect the name tags, and place star stickers on the Attendance Charts. Then collect the *Singer's Editions*, allowing the main characters to take their books home if they want to practice. Interact with the children as they leave. Ask the children who are still in the room to help you clean up and put things away.

Review

Meet with the primary leaders and helpers, and develop a rehearsal schedule for the main characters. (These characters should practice before and after the session for no more than five to ten minutes at a time.) Assess where you are in the costuming, tree-making, and sign-making processes. Adjust the plans for the Drama Centers as needed. Prepare to paint the backdrop in the next rehearsal. Assign responsibilities for Session Five as needed.

Notes

Session Five

Preparation

Materials
- ☐ Cassette player and *Listening Tape*
- ☐ *Singer's Editions*
- ☐ The Singers' Card File
- ☐ Star stickers
- ☐ Name tags
- ☐ Backdrop and prop supplies
- ☐ Painting smocks or shirts
- ☐ Supplies for Drama Centers
- ☐ Orff instruments
- ☐ Pencils
- ☐ Progress Bulletin Board materials

Prepare Backdrop and Prop Supplies
See "Create the Stable Scene" on pages 37-38 for information about the backdrop. If you plan to paint the backdrop, have men's old shirts on hand to use as painting smocks. In advance, ask an adult or youth to pencil in lanterns, a dove, planking marks, and so forth on the backdrop. Gather supplies for making the wooden storage boxes, gift boxes, lanterns, and other props. (See "Costuming and Props," page 41.)

Set Up Drama Centers
Set up the Drama Centers, and review the supply of materials. Replace items as needed.

Review Session Plans
Study the plans for this session, and work toward maintaining a smooth flow from one activity to the next.

Into the Story

Welcome the Children
Play the recording of "7b. Hush! Hush!" as you welcome the children. Encourage the children to find a group and participate in an activity. Work with Young Joseph on his solo in "7a. Hush! Hush!" Enlist helpers to meet with other children to read through their lines. Update the Singers' Card File.

Gathering Activities
Ask helpers to space themselves around the room and encourage the children to work on word games (see "Get Ready," page 9); to memorize song texts; to complete their costumes as necessary; and to listen to the recording of *What Child Was This?* as they follow the music in their *Singer's Editions*.

Continue practicing the Orff-style accompaniment to "7b. Hush! Hush!"

Warm Up Voices
As the children move to their rehearsal places, lead them in singing the warm-up on page 8. Model clear vowel sounds and consonants for the children.

Continue using phrases of the songs that need special attention as warm-ups.

Introduce the Story: The Kings, Matthew 2:1-2

Have the children playing Mary, Joseph, Angels, Shepherds, and Kings stand. Ask, "Which of these characters is not mentioned in Luke 2:1-20?" (the Kings.) Find the scriptures on page 1 of the *Singer's Edition*, and read together the lesson from Matthew.

Matthew writes of kings who followed a large star that led them to the Christ Child. The kings brought three valuable gifts to Jesus—gold, frankincense, and myrrh. Share with the group that the kings are sometimes called "wise men" and "Magi." The Bible does not tell us how many kings there were, but ancient folk stories suggest that there were three. In these tales, the "three wise men" from Persia were named Balthasar, Gaspar, and Melchior.

Historians say that it probably took a very long time for the kings to travel to Bethlehem. They may have arrived as much as two years after Jesus was born. We traditionally include them in the Nativity scene because they remind us that Jesus was born for all persons, no matter what their economic, educational, or racial status. All peoples are called to worship Jesus.

Into the Songs

Introduce "7b. Hush! Hush!"

Play the recording of "7b. Hush! Hush!" as the children follow along in their music. Have them close their books, and teach measures 1-11 phrase by phrase. Once the children are secure with the text and pitches, add the motions found on page 48. Begin to sing the song in a two-part, *a cappella* canon using a helper to direct Part II.

Review All Songs Learned So Far

To enable the children to get a sense of the musical's flow, sing through each song—do not stop the singers unless they are unable to sing a part. Assist the soloists as needed. Review: "2. Taxes, Taxes," "3. We've Come So Far," "4. All the Sky Was Filled with Angels," "5. Born this Night," and "7b. Hush! Hush!" Make a note of which sections need work and which are already memorized.

Progress Bulletin Board

Place leaves on the trees as appropriate.

Into the Drama

Scene Groups and Drama Centers

During this session, the Drama Leader and other leaders will continue to work on lines and blocking with the three scene groups: Kings and Servants; Shepherds 1, 2, and 3 and Angels 1 and 2; Young Joseph, Old Joseph, and Mary.

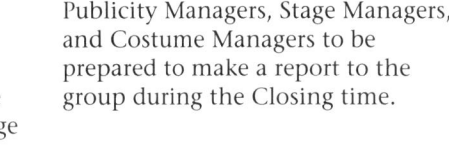

All other children will paint the backdrop, construct props, finish the palm tree, or meet with adult helpers to plan publicity, costume coordination, stage setting, and so forth. Ask the children who are serving as

Publicity Managers, Stage Managers, and Costume Managers to be prepared to make a report to the group during the Closing time.

Closing

Bring the Children Together
Tell the children that at the next rehearsal they will memorize more of the song texts, do a run-through of the musical, and work on the movements for some of the songs. Thank them for their hard work, and ask them to thank the helpers who have worked with them. Let the Managers make their reports, and facilitate any group decisions that need to be made after hearing the reports.

Pray Together
Lead the children in praying the following prayer phrase by phrase.

Dear God, we thank you for the baby who was born to save us all. Give us your peace and joy as we continue to lift up our voices and sing praises to you. Amen.

Sing with the children the chorus of "5. Born This Night."

Name Tags, Attendance Charts, and Rehearsal with Soloist
Collect name tags, place stickers on the Attendance Charts, and collect the *Singer's Editions*. Allow the main characters to take their books home with them if they want or need extra practice. Work with the soloist scheduled for a brief rehearsal after the session.

Review
Review the plans the publicity team has made, and make a list of the supplies needed. Notify the adult working with the Costume Manager that all costumes should be ready

by Session Seven. Notify the adult working with the Stage Manager that the sets and props should be completed by Session Eight. Arrange to meet with the Drama Leader and Music Leader to review the songs and scenes that need the most work. Personally thank all the helpers and leaders.

Notes

Session Six

OVERVIEW

Preparation
Gather Publicity Supplies
Review Supplies for Drama Centers
Prepare Consonant Squares
Review Session Plans

Into the Story
Welcome the Children
Gathering Activities
Warm Up Voices
Into the Story: Tell One Another the Story

Into the Songs
Memorize "4. All the Sky Was Filled with Angels"

Review "5. Born This Night"
Review "7b. Hush! Hush!"
Review "3. We've Come So Far"
Begin to Memorize "9b. What Child Is This"
Progress Bulletin Board

Into the Drama
Scene Groups and Drama Centers

Closing
Bring the Children Together
Pray Together
Name Tags, Attendance Charts, and Rehearsal with Soloist
Review

Preparation

Materials
❏ Cassette player and *Listening Tape*
❏ *Singer's Editions*
❏ The Singers' Card File
❏ Star stickers
❏ Name tags
❏ Backdrop and prop supplies
❏ Supplies for Drama Centers
❏ Publicity materials
❏ N-S-E-W Bull's-Eye Chart
❏ Consonant Squares
❏ Orff instruments
❏ Pencils
❏ Progress Bulletin Board materials

Gather Publicity Supplies
Collect supplies such as posterboard, permanent markers, and crayons in accordance with the children's publicity plans. As much as possible, let the Publicity Manager gather and organize the supplies. This child could also help address envelopes to the local newspaper, arrange for a helper to photograph the cast, and make phone calls.

Review Supplies for Drama Centers
The children should be completing their projects in this session or the next. Move supplies among the three centers as needed.

Prepare Consonant Squares
Using the illustration on page 8, create the Consonant Squares.

Review Session Plans
Review the plans for this session to ensure smooth transitions.

Into the Story

Welcome the Children
Personally greet the children as they arrive, and help them find their name tags. Encourage them to find a group and participate in an activity. Update the Singers' Card File.

Gathering Activities
Provide activity areas and helpers to assist the children in memorizing the texts using word games or work sheets such as the Word Search on page 18 of the *Singer's Edition*;

listening to the recording; practicing the song movements; and rehearsing the Orff-style accompaniment. Work with the soloists as scheduled.

Warm Up Voices
As the children move to their rehearsal places, lead them in singing the warm-up on page 8. Continue using phrases of the songs that need special attention as warm-ups.

Into the Story: Tell One Another the Story
Ask the children to share the story of Luke 2:1-20 and Matthew 2:1-2 with the group. Remind them that we should tell others about Christ and that the story of Christ's birth is one of the stories they can share with others.

Into the Songs

Memorize "4. All the Sky Was Filled with Angels"
Work on memorization, enunciation, and clear vowels. Use the N-S-E-W Bull's-Eye Chart to remind the children visually of the "north-south mouth." Ask some of the children to hold the Consonant Squares and to raise them each time their ending consonant is sung. Teach the divisi of the last measure of Part II (measure 37). Sing the final C section again, listening for security of text and melody.

Review "5. Born This Night"
Sing the song in its entirety. Then rehearse the two-part ending (measures 35 and 36). Review the text and work on memorization. Use the N-S-E-W Bull's-Eye Chart and Consonant Squares as visual aids.

Review "7b. Hush! Hush!"
Assign the three canon parts according to character (Part I: Kings; Part II: Servants; Part III: Shepherds), or divide the choir according to how the singers will be standing. Sing the canon by memory.

Review "3. We've Come So Far"
Continue working with soloists and chorus. Sing the song in its entirety, and then work with the choir on the letter C section and measures 60-65. Use the N-S-E-W Bull's-Eye Chart and Consonant Squares as visual aids.

Begin to Memorize "9b. What Child Is This"
Ask the children to come sit in a circle with you. Try to sing stanza 1 and the refrain of "9b. What Child

Is This" from memory. Correct any memorization problems, and then rehearse stanzas 2 and 3. Memorize the text in a variety of ways—speak the text in rhythm; sing a phrase and have the children repeat it; play the Musical Memorization game. To play the game, have the children sit on the floor in a circle. As you move around the outside of the circle, touch a child's head as you sing one phrase. The child then sings the phrase as a solo. Move around the circle, giving each child a chance to sing a phrase from the first three stanzas. Help any child who has difficulty by singing with him or her.

Progress Bulletin Board
Add the "Memorized" leaves as appropriate.

Into the Drama

Scene Groups and Drama Centers
This is the last time the Drama Leader and other leaders will work on lines and blocking with the three scene groups: Kings and Servants; Shepherds 1, 2, and 3 and Angels 1 and 2; Young Joseph, Old

Joseph, and Mary. All other children will paint the backdrop, construct props, finish the palm tree, or work on publicity. Ask helpers to assist small groups of chorus members with their role characterizations. Help them decide how to move and act appropriately

for the age and occupation of their characters. Review the motions of "2. Taxes, Taxes," "4. All the Sky Was Filled with Angels," and "7b. Hush! Hush!" with each of the small groups.

Closing

Bring the Children Together
Thank the children for their hard work. Tell them that next week during the "Into the Drama" time, they will practice staging and singing the songs in position. Everyone should practice his or her characterizations at home.

Mention that there is one song the group has not yet sung. They will sing it at the next rehearsal. This song is a "reprise" or "repetition" of "5. Born This Night." They will also learn how to move from the quiet song, "7b. Hush! Hush!" to the joyful reprise of "Born This Night."

Discuss any publicity details that need the attention of the group. Remind the children that at the next session they will try on their costumes for a costume check. Answer any questions the children may have. Make a note of those questions that need to be answered by others.

Pray Together
Pray the prayer below.

> *Dear Prince of Peace, come into our hearts today and fill us with your peace. Help us to share what we are learning about you with others. Now, Jesus, we ask that you strengthen us for the tasks ahead. In your name we pray. Amen.*

Name Tags, Attendance Charts, and Rehearsal with Soloist
Collect the name tags, place stickers on the Attendance Charts, and then collect the *Singer's Editions*. Allow main characters to keep their books. Speak to the children individually as they leave, and encourage those who are having difficulty memorizing the words. Work with the soloist scheduled for a brief rehearsal after the session.

Review
Meet with the other leaders, and prepare to do a costume check at the next session. Review plans for staging the chorus, making any necessary adjustments. Follow through on answering the questions that you could not answer during the rehearsal. If possible, contact the children who asked these questions when you know the answers. Assess the children's progress in painting the sets, memorizing the music, and so forth. Make adjustments to Session Seven as needed.

Notes

Session Seven

Preparation

Materials
- ❑ Cassette player and *Listening Tape*
- ❑ *Singer's Editions*
- ❑ The Singers' Card File
- ❑ Star stickers
- ❑ Name tags
- ❑ Supplies to complete sets, props, and costumes
- ❑ Newsprint
- ❑ Permanent markers
- ❑ Masking tape
- ❑ Publicity materials
- ❑ Orff instruments
- ❑ Pencils
- ❑ Progress Bulletin Board materials

Meet with the Pastor
Meet with the pastor to finalize plans for the worship service and to review the order of worship in which the musical is to be presented. Ask the pastor to talk with the children during the rehearsal about how to be worship leaders.

Print Order of Worship on Newsprint
After meeting with the pastor, write the order of worship on newsprint. Tape it on a wall in the rehearsal area.

Prepare Costumes for Fitting
Arrange to have adults assist in fitting costumes during the "Gathering Activities" time.

Prepare the Presentation Area
Prepare the presentation area for the blocking drill later in this session. Move furniture as necessary, and mark the area with masking tape.

Finalize Publicity Plans
Finalize the publicity strategy. Arrange to have posters and adhesive tape available.

Review Session Plans
Study the session plans, and be prepared to stage the chorus.

Into the Service

Welcome the Children
Greet the children individually as they arrive, and help them find their name tags. Encourage them to find a group and participate in an activity. Update the Singers' Card File.

Gathering Activities
Provide activity areas and helpers to assist the children in memorizing the texts using word games or work sheets; listening to the recording; practicing the song movements; and rehearsing the Orff-style accompaniment. Work with the soloists as scheduled. Fit costumes and assign props as needed.

Warm Up Voices
As the children move to their rehearsal places, lead them in singing the warm-up on page 8. Continue using phrases of the songs that need special attention as warm-ups.

Tell the Story: Order of Worship
Show the children the order of worship you have prepared. Ask them if they are listening or talking to God during each act of the worship service. Ask them what usually happens during the sermon. (We listen and learn more about Jesus and how to live our lives.) Tell them that they will be teaching people about Jesus' birth and how to live the life of a follower of Jesus by presenting *What Child Was This?* during the Proclamation of the Word (the sermon time). They are reminding the congregation that Jesus' birth is very important to us and that we need to tell others about Jesus.

Live the Story: Being Worship Leaders
Introduce your pastor (or other worship leader) to the children. Ask the pastor to tell the children about how he or she first learned of Jesus' birth. Discuss how *What Child Was This?* will be presented in worship. Include the date and time, and where in the service the musical will occur. Tell the children that they will have an important leadership role in the worship service that Sunday.

Ask them who else serves as worship leaders during the worship service. Briefly discuss the roles these persons play in worship. Tell the children that these people plan, rehearse, and lead the congregation in praising God through music and the spoken word. Make sure you lift up the choir director, organist, scripture readers, ushers, acolytes, and any others who serve as worship leaders.

Into the Songs

Introduce "8. Born This Night" (Reprise)
Have Young Joseph say his lines prior to the singing of "7b. Hush! Hush!" (*Singer's Edition*, page 13). Sing "7b. Hush! Hush!" very quietly, and then lead the children in joyously singing "8. Born This Night." Ask, "Who remembers what a reprise is?" (A repetition.) Practice "7b. Hush! Hush!" again, adding the movements and recessional of Kings, Servants, and Shepherds.

Review Songs
Review any songs or sections of songs that you feel need extra work. Tell the children exactly which sections of music you would like to rehearse. Work only on those specific spots in the songs.

Progress Bulletin Board
Review the Progress Bulletin Board, and add any new leaves. Note how much work remains before the songs are "Ready to Go!"

Into the Drama

Display Publicity Posters and Props
Group the children into small teams with an adult assistant, and divide the publicity posters and masking tape among them. Instruct the children to complete the poster preparation by attaching the masking tape. Offer suggestions on where the posters may be displayed. Have the children move to the presentation area after posting their posters.

Stage the Chorus
Stage the chorus beginning with the last song, working backward to the first song. As they rehearse in the presentation area for the first time, the chorus members will be very excited! Starting with "7b. Hush! Hush!" and "8. Born This Night" (Reprise) will help them focus. Working the order of the songs backward will also make staging interesting and fun! Remind the children to be in character at all times.

Share with them that blocking involves where you stand, sit, or move. Summarize the dialogue that occurs before each song, and tell them the name of the song as they are positioned. (Add the movements they have practiced.) Correct any note or text problems. When you sense that the children need a break, ask them to sit and join you in several sets of "Simon Says."

Blocking Drill
Do a blocking drill in which the children practice moving from position to position without singing. Place the cast members in the proper positions for "1. Overture" and "2. Taxes, Taxes." Block the songs in the order they occur in the musical. Make suggestions for moving smoothly from position to position.

Complete Sets, Costumes, and Props
Return to the primary rehearsal space. Complete all sets, costumes, and props.

Closing

Bring the Children Together
Ask the children to come sit together. Sing "9b. What Child Is This" from memory. Thank the children for their attention and cooperation during the rehearsal. Tell them that they will have a "technical" rehearsal the next time—they will be practicing with the sets in place, with any microphones that you will be using, and with the instrumentalists. Share with them that you will be stopping and starting and sometimes going to the beginning of a section to help all feel comfortable with their part in the musical.

Pray Together
Pray the prayer below.

> *Dear God, thank you for giving each of us a talent to share. We ask that you help us to use our talents so others will to come to know you. Help us to remember that Jesus is "Christ the King, whom shepherds guard and angels sing." Help us hasten to "bring him laud, the babe, the son of Mary." In Jesus' name we pray, Amen.*

Name Tags, Attendance Charts, and Rehearsal with Soloist
Collect name tags, and thank each child for his or her work during the session. Mention something each child did that made you proud. Help the singers place stickers on their Attendance Charts, and let them take their books home if desired. Work with the soloist scheduled for a brief rehearsal after the session.

Review
Meet with the primary leaders and review the blocking drill. Work out any problems that were discovered during rehearsal. Plan to work with the Costume, Stage, and Publicity Managers before the next session so that these children will be confident leaders. Make plans to remind instrumentalists of the time and place of Sessions Eight and Nine rehearsals.

Notes

Session Eight

Preparation

Materials

❏ Cassette player and *Listening Tape*
❏ *Singer's Editions*
❏ The Singers' Card File
❏ Star stickers
❏ Name tags
❏ Sets, props, and costumes
❏ Newsprint
❏ Permanent markers
❏ Hymnals
❏ Construction paper
❏ Hole punch
❏ Ribbon
❏ Orff instruments
❏ Camel/sleigh bells
❏ Order of Worship
❏ Music stands, chairs, and music scores for instrumentalists
❏ Progress Bulletin Board materials

Collect Supplies for the Special Invitation
On a piece of newsprint, write: *"What Child Was This? A musical by John Horman, Date: _____, Time: _____, Place: _____.* Please come worship with us as [name of group] presents this musical in worship."

Prepare to use this invitation during the "Gathering Activity" time.

Contact Instrumentalists
Remind instrumentalists when and where to come for rehearsal.

Ready Presentation Space
Set up the presentation space, including stands and chairs for the instrumentalists. Place the handbell tables in a location where they can be seen by the conductor and the congregation, but not in the congregation's direct sight line of the presentation.

Place Sets and Props in the Presentation Area
Although all of the sets may not be quite completed, place the risers, palm tree, and other large set props in the presentation area. Try to complete all the props before the session begins.

Post a Copy of the Order of Worship
Place a copy of the worship bulletin in a visible location so the children can look at it.

Mark Hymnals
Mark the Hymnals so the children will be able to find hymns easily. Use scraps of construction paper, ribbons, and so forth from the Drama Centers to mark places in the Hymnals.

Collect Camel/Sleigh Bells
Gather camel or sleigh bells for use in "6. Procession of the Kings." If your church does not have these instruments, contact a local school or church.

Review Session Plans
Study the plans for this session, and aim for a smooth flow from one activity to the next.

Into the Service

Welcome the Children
As the children arrive, play the recording of a song that needs work. Greet the children, and help them find their name tags. Encourage them to participate in the "Gathering Activity." Update the Singers' Card File.

Gathering Activity: Make Invitations
Make invitations to the worship service on pieces of construction paper. (Use the Special Invitation as a reference.) After the children have written on the paper, let them fold the invitation in half and punch a hole through the middle of the sides opposite the fold. Thread a piece of ribbon through the hole and tie it in a bow. Ask the children to take their invitations to friends or neighbors and invite them to attend the musical presentation.

Review the Service
Review the order of worship with the children. Distribute hymnals, and rehearse music that will be used in worship on the day of the presentation. Choose helpers to collect the hymnals.

Warm Up Voices
Sing the stanza of "9b. What Child Is This" on "loo," switching to "lah" for the refrain.

Into the Songs and Drama

Purpose of Session
The purpose of this session is a technical rehearsal, and you will be stopping and starting the children several times. Correct the text, notes, flubbed lines of dialogue, and help the accompanist and instrumentalists. Tell the children that each time you stop and start, the musical will be getting better! Show them where they will find their costumes for the dress rehearsal. Move into the presentation space, and take positions for the beginning of the musical.

Run-through of Musical
Run the musical in its entirety, stopping and reviewing as needed. Work on balance between the accompaniment and the children and also smooth transitions between songs and lines. Watch the blocking closely so that each child can be clearly seen and heard. Rehearse sections that need work, including lines, movements, and blocking. Add the bells to "6. Procession the Kings." During the processional, the chorus members should pantomime in character when they see the Kings coming. Remind the singers that their actions should enhance rather than detract from the entrance of the Kings and Servants.

Questions?
Answer any questions the children may have. They may help you solve some of the problems!

Run-through of Sections
Run specific sections of the musical. Review those that need a little more practice. Listen for clarity of text and for good singing tones.

Thank the Instrumentalists
Thank the instrumentalists for playing for the musical, and introduce them to the children. Remind the players of the time and place of the next rehearsal. Arrange to meet with them separately if extra rehearsal time is needed.

Progress Bulletin Board
Add leaves to the palm trees as appropriate. All of the leaves except "Ready To Go!" should be attached by the end of this session.

Closing

Bring the Children Together
If time allows, play a word game. Thank the children for their work, and remind them that the next session is the dress rehearsal. Everyone will be wearing costumes, and once the musical has begun, you will not stop it. Review publicity plans as needed. Remind the Stage and Costume Managers to meet with the adult helpers after the rehearsal to discuss how to organize their areas for the dress rehearsal.

Pray Together
Pray the following prayer.

Dear Lord, what fun it is to sing and work together! Thank you for allowing us to learn more about the birth of Jesus. Help us to remember that we should always lift up our voices and sing your praise. Amen.

Name Tags, Attendance Charts, and Rehearsal with Soloist
Let the children take their name tags home today, and be sure they put star stickers on their Attendance Charts. Allow the children to take their *Singer's Editions* home if they want more practice. Praise each child for something he or she did extremely well today. If a soloist was scheduled for a brief rehearsal, meet with him or her. Adult helpers should assist the Costume and Stage Managers in cleaning up the area, moving equipment, and so forth.

Review
Meet with the primary leaders to review today's session. Adjust the set placement and blocking if needed.

Session Nine

Preparation

Materials
❏ *Singer's Editions*
❏ The Singers' Card File
❏ Star stickers
❏ Sets, props, and costumes
❏ Orff instruments
❏ Camel/sleigh bells
❏ Music stands, chairs, and music scores for the instrumentalists
❏ Progress Bulletin Board materials

Ready Presentation Area
Put the sets and props in place so the musical can be rehearsed exactly as it will be presented in worship. Set up the space for the instrumentalists as well.

Ready Costumes
Place the costumes where the children will find and return them on the day of the presentation.

Consider hanging each costume on a marked hanger. Collect odds and ends in a grocery bag marked with each child's name.

Plan for a Snack
If you would like to have a special snack at the close of the rehearsal, ask several parents to provide fruit, popcorn, or other snack food.

Into the Service

Welcome the Children
Greet the children, and place stars on their Attendance Charts. Update the Singers' Card File.

Costume the Children
Enlisting the help of other leaders, assist the children in finding their costumes and dressing for the rehearsal.

Assemble the Children in Presentation Area
When the children are costumed, move quietly into the presentation area. Have them take their places

for the beginning of the musical. Tell the children that they will do a complete run-through without stopping. Ask them to hold all questions until after this first run-through. Assure them that you will then answer their questions and share the notes you have taken during the first run-through.

Explain the importance of cooperation. Seeing everything put together will be exciting for them, but you need their very best behavior and help to make everything work well.

Remind the children where in the worship service their presentation will take place by showing them the order of worship posted on the wall. Encourage them to listen carefully to the story as the characters are speaking so that they can react to what is happening in the ways the story suggests. Tell them that after they have sung the closing song, they will leave their costumes on but go into the congregation and be seated until the end of the service.

Into the Dress Rehearsal

Review and Focus

Sing all of the songs one time, having children move quickly and quietly to their places for each song. Try not to worry about mistakes; just quietly fix the problem spots and continue. Help them focus by asking them to sit still, breathing in and out quietly several times. Then pray: "Lord, please help us tell the story of your birth. You have helped us to fill the past rehearsals with fun and work, now fill our lungs and voices with the joy of your newborn Son. Fill our minds and hearts with praise for you. We pray this in Jesus' name. Amen."

Do the First Run-through and Review

Make sure the children are in position for the beginning of the musical. As the story progresses, give as few directions as possible. Take notes on anything that does not flow smoothly or work well, in addition to those parts or persons that deserve special praise. Try not to stop, and save all comments and suggestions for after the first run-through.

After the first run-through, review your notes with the children. Begin with those portions that went particularly well, and then alert them to anything needing improvement. Answer any questions the children may have, and prepare for the second run-through.

Do the Second Run-through and Review

Have the children go to their beginning places, and do a second complete run-through. Again, work toward stopping as little as possible, but feel free to stop and make corrections if there seems to be a major problem. After the second run-through, gather the children centerstage and thank them for their cooperation and hard work. If you have additional notes, review them with the children quickly.

Closing

Prepare the Children for the Presentation

Acknowledge those children with the best rehearsal attendance records. Affirm once again all the work they have put into preparing the musical. Make sure they know where to gather before the presentation and what time they are to be there. A short note to parents, particularly if your group has several younger children, would be appropriate.

Pray Together

Lead the children in a prayer that captures the experience that you have had together while preparing *What Child Was This?* Offer thanks to God for allowing you to learn about the birth of Jesus.

Complete Progress Bulletin Board

Attach any final "Ready to Go!" leaves to the palm trees.

Gather the Costumes

Ask the children to return their costumes to the appropriate place.

They should hang the costumes as they found them earlier today. Invite the children to have refreshments.

Thank Children and Parents

As the children prepare to leave, thank the families and children for participating in the musical. Call the children during the week or write short notes thanking them for their work during the preparation of the musical.

Notes

Session Ten

OVERVIEW OF PRESENTATION

Preparation
   Prepare the Sets, Props, and Costumes
   Prepare Yourself
   Copy the Bulletin Insert

Into the Service
   Welcome the Children

Review the Songs
Pray with the Children
Direct the Children Quietly to Their
   Places
After the Service

Preparation

Materials
❑ Sets, props, and costumes
❑ Percussion instruments
❑ Music stands, chairs, and
   music scores for
   instrumentalists

Prepare the Sets, Props, and Costumes
Check and double-check all of the set components and the costumes.

It is very important that everything be ready and in place before the children arrive.

Prepare Yourself
Excited children need to be surrounded by calm, prepared adults. As you prepare with prayer, think through the entire story. In your mind, picture the children moving into their places; going through the narration, songs and movement; and then dispersing into the congregation. Picture the congregation and its eagerness to receive the children's gift of a story. Thank God that you have had the opportunity to lead this musical experience.

Copy the Bulletin Insert
Make copies of the bulletin insert found on page 88, and place these in the worship bulletins.

Into the Service

Welcome the Children
As the children arrive, calmly help them into their costumes. When they are dressed, have them sit quietly until everyone is ready.

Review the Songs
Quickly sing through each song, reminding the children of any special places that need attention.

Pray with the Children
Ask the children to bow their heads for a few minutes of silent prayer. Encourage them to think through the story—their lines, songs, and movement. They should also picture themselves doing their very best. Close your prayer time with the following prayer.

Our songs are prepared, our lines are prepared, our movements are prepared. So come now, Lord Jesus, as a newborn child to make us joyful; as a teacher and miracle worker to help us live each day; and as our risen Savior to bring us eternal life. Send your Spirit, and fill the hearts of those in the congregation with peace. "Glory, glory in the highest! It is of God's peace we sing. Glory, glory in the highest! Tidings of great joy we bring." Amen.

Direct the Children Quietly to Their Places
Lead the children quietly to their places and let the story begin!

After the Service
Spend a few minutes in a prayer of thanks. Thank God for the children and for the gifts God has given you and the helpers to enable you to lead the children.

   Contact each person involved in the musical, and thank them personally for participating.

Get Set

Purpose of the Sets

- To help the cast and congregation imagine themselves in another time and place
- To set the atmosphere for congregations as they enter the sanctuary
- To help tell the story through visual representation

Materials for Carpentry Shop, Chorus Area, Shepherds' Hillside

- ❏ Wooden table, bench, partially completed manger
- ❏ Choral risers or benches
- ❏ Riser with dark covering

Instructions for Creating the Sets

Plan the set to fit in the available space in your presentation area. Finalize the scene design and complete the basic construction before painting begins.

Always have an adult present when children are working on the set.

Headdresses, halos, crowns, girdles, props, backdrop, and "TAXES" signs will be made by the children in Drama Centers. Use adult helpers to set up supplies and provide instruction in the Drama Center area. Allow the children to enjoy being creative.

The basic set consists of:

- **Old Joseph's carpentry shop:** A wooden table and bench and a partially completed manger. (The manger will need to be completed easily by Old Joseph during the production.)
- **Central stable scene:** One or two benches, a backdrop, a swaddled baby doll, and a bale of hay.
- **Shepherds' hillside:** A riser painted a dark color or covered by a dark rug or piece of material.
- **Chorus area:** Use multiple risers to facilitate a good line of sight between director and singers. If your church doesn't have risers, consider borrowing some from a local school; or stage the children so that some are seated on a long picnic bench with others standing behind them.
- A **paper palm tree** positioned between the chorus risers and the shepherds' hillside.

Materials for Manger

- ❏ Pieces of plywood or scrap lumber cut to size
- ❏ Four tree branches of the same thickness, at least 30" in length
- ❏ Saw, hammer, nails, and drill
- ❏ Two large bolts
- ❏ Screws, washers, and nuts
- ❏ Two large hinges
- ❏ Sandpaper
- ❏ Dark paint or stain

Manger

Using the illustration here, create a manger out of pieces of plywood and tree branches. (Check to see if your church already has a manger. If you live near a farming area, you may be able to borrow an old wooden manger.)

The instructions are designed to make the manger easy to store and transport if you are taking the musical "on the road." If storage is not a concern, you can nail the manger together.

1. Cross two of the branches to make one set of legs. Drill a hole through each where they meet, and bolt together. Do the same with the other set of branches.

2. Cut two pieces of plywood, approximately 24" x 12", and join them together on one long side with two hinges. This will create the sides of the manger.

3. Nail the short ends of the manger sides to the inside of the legs above the bolts. (This will allow you to fold the manger for storage.)

4. Decide how wide you want the manger to be (14" to 18"). Measure, and then cut two triangles out of plywood to create the ends of the manger. Drill a hole in the top of two of the end piece sides. Screw the end pieces into the outer top sides of the branch legs.

5. Check for rough edges, and sand as needed so the children will not hurt themselves when carrying the manger. Paint or stain the wood a dark color. To transport the manger, simply unscrew the end pieces and fold the manger.

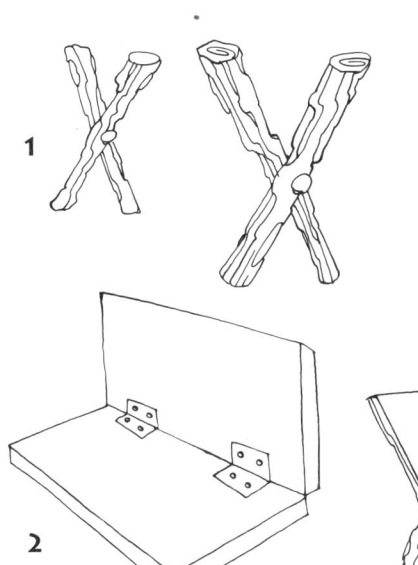

Materials for Stable Scene
Stable Option 1

- ❏ One or more portable room dividers or chalkboards
- ❏ Heavy paper or cardboard
- ❏ Tempera paints in various colors
- ❏ Staples, tacks, or clear packing tape
- ❏ Paintbrushes
- ❏ Pencils
- ❏ Clean-up supplies

Create the Stable Scene

Option 1: Depending on the amount of presentation space available, cover one or more room dividers or chalkboards with a painted stable backdrop. Include in the scene bales of hay, lanterns, and perhaps even a dove, sheep, or cow. Paint the backdrop on heavy paper or light cardboard, which can be easily tacked to the dividers.

Option 2: If you hope to take your musical "on the road" or if you see a need for a backdrop that can be reused and easily stored, buy two solid ivory or white flat sheets for each divider and sew them together on three sides to create a divider "pillowcase." Paint the scenes on the "cases" and slip them over the dividers. Fold to store. To create a basic backdrop without painting, use solid dark tan or brown sheets to imitate walls. For even more portability, create lightweight stands for the backdrop or "cases." Use three lengths of PVC pipe cut to fit your backdrops or "cases"; two 90-degree PVC connectors; and two banner stands.

Option 3: Nail weathered construction pallets together on their ends to create a V-shaped, free-standing backdrop for the stable. Contact a local nursery or construction company to ask if any pallets are available. To complete the stable, hang pieces of old rope from the pallets, and add a bale of hay.

Let the children who volunteer as Stage Managers help design the set, make sure it fits in the space allotted, and set it up in the proper place. Under your supervision, allow them to set up (and put away) the set for each session and for the presentation. Ask if any of the children would like to go with you to the store to purchase supplies. If so, arrange this outing with the parents.

Create a Paper Palm Tree

Ask a carpet store to save two or three cardboard carpet tubes for you. Using duct tape, tape the tubes together to create a circumference equal to a large Christmas tree stand. Wrap the tubes in brown paper or brown burlap, and put the tube "tree trunk" securely in the stand. Make four or more palm leaves. For each palm leaf, cut two large palm leaf forms out of green bulletin board paper, and tape a wire down the center of the wrong side of the leaf. Glue the wrong side of a second paper leaf to the wrong side of the leaf with the wire. Tape or wire the leaf into the outside top edges of the carpet tube. Bend the leaf to a pleasing shape. Cover the base of the tree in a green sheet or a piece of outdoor carpeting.

Costuming and Props

Purpose of Costuming and Props
- To enable the cast members to develop character roles
- To aid in setting the story

Materials
- ❏ T-shirt for each child and primary adult leader
- ❏ Liquid dye in spray bottles (earth-tone colors)
- ❏ Assorted lengths and colors of cloth
- ❏ Plastic jewels, old costume jewelry
- ❏ Snippets of fabric trim
- ❏ Glue
- ❏ Caps or felt hats
- ❏ Inexpensive plastic headbands
- ❏ Garland
- ❏ Large boxes with lids
- ❏ Pieces of rope
- ❏ Small boxes
- ❏ Pencils
- ❏ Brown wrapping paper
- ❏ Shiny gold/silver wrapping paper or spray paint
- ❏ Cylindrical, pressed-paper containers
- ❏ X-acto knife
- ❏ Black spray paint
- ❏ Small flashlights
- ❏ Wire coat hangers and wire cutters
- ❏ Posterboard and permanent markers
- ❏ Tree branches, trimmed

Instructions for Costuming the Cast

The chorus will work in Drama Centers to create headdresses and dyed T-shirt costumes. Children portraying special roles will wear long, loose vests over their T-shirts and will have a prop, such as a halo or walking stick. Pace the work so that the costumes and character props are finished completely by Session Seven. Old Joseph, Mary, Young Joseph, and the Kings may wear traditional biblical costumes. Check to see what biblical costumes the church already has, and have them ready by Session Seven.

Have helpers construct or alter the remaining costumes, and ask that these be made available to the children no later than Session Seven. Consult reference materials for additional information and ideas about clothes worn during Jesus' time. The children who volunteer to be Costume Managers should help keep a record of each person's costume. With the aid of adults, let them mark names in the costumes and hang and store the costumes for rehearsals and the presentation. Enable them to make simple repairs and to create special costume props as needed.

Costumes

Each child will wear a dyed T-shirt, girdle, headdress, and dark slacks or tights/leggings with dark shoes. While adult volunteers will dye the T-shirts and create the vests for the Angels, Shepherds, Kings, Servants, Mary, Old Joseph, and Young Joseph, the children will create their own headdresses, girdles, crowns, or halos. When choosing fabric, pick neutral colors if possible, especially for Mary, Joseph, the Servants, and Old Joseph. The Kings should wear more colorful material, and you may glue plastic jewels on the cloth if desired. Make crowns out of posterboard wrapped in shiny paper or painted gold or silver, and glue plastic jewels into place.

- **Dyed T-shirts:** Ask each child to bring a white adult-size T-shirt. Find a place where you can use a hose and dye without worrying about making a mess. Outdoors works best. Place the shirt on a hanger and soak it with a hose. Then, use a spray bottle filled in advance with the desired color dye and a fabric medium to apply the color to the shoulders and the collar area of the shirt. The dye will "run" or bleed down the length of the shirt, forming patterns as it goes. Adding water to the shirt will cause the color to lighten, and more dye causes it to darken. The best effect is a combination of light and dark, much like the traditional tie-dyed look. Use earth-tone colors in browns, blues, purples, greens, and so forth, but only one color per shirt! Dry the T-shirt thoroughly and iron as needed. Make one T-shirt in each color for the adult leaders to wear to the first two sessions.

- **Vests:** Use white material for the Angels' vests and brown or gray material for vests for the Shepherds, Servants, Young Joseph, and Old Joseph. Use brightly colored material for the Kings. Measure the children from the back of their necks to their ankles. You will need twice that length of material for the vest. Estimate the width so that the vests will fit loosely on the children.
  1. Fold the material right sides together, matching the selvage edges, and cut across the fold.
  2. To create the two front panels of the vest, take one of the pieces you just cut and cut it again lengthwise.
  3. Sew the side seams, leaving eight inches at the top for the arm holes.
  4. Fold under two inches of each of the front center panels, matching wrong side to wrong side. Sew a seam 1/2-inch from the fold, and cut off the excess to use as a girdle.
  5. Match the shoulder pieces and seam them, gathering the shoulders to three inches in width.
  6. Iron. Add decorations as appropriate to the character.

- **Girdle (Belt):** Make this item from folded cloth, vinyl, fake leather, or other material. For the Kings' costumes, use fabric paint to "embroider" the girdle or glue plastic jewels and metal ornaments on it. Girdles may be wrapped over T-shirts with the vests hanging free, or the vests can be wrapped across the front of the body with the girdle tied on top.

- **Headdresses:**
  Option 1: Cut a square of material and drape it loosely on the head. Bind the square with twisted or braided strips of cloth.
  Option 2: Find an old cap or felt hat without a brim and wrap a strip of cloth eighteen inches wide and two to three yards long around the hat to create a turban.
  Option 3: Cut a strip of material, and tie it around the child's head like a sweat band.

- **Halos:** Buy inexpensive plastic headbands, and glue twisted or braided lengths of garland on them. Glue the ends of the garland securely.

- **Crowns:** Cut posterboard to the desired shape and cover with shiny gold or silver wrapping paper or spray paint. Glue on decorations such as plastic jewels, old costume jewelry, or snippets of fabric trims.

Props

Young Joseph may carry a box or walking stick as he and Mary "travel" to Bethlehem. At least three of the Servants should carry one decorated chest each. These chests will contain the gifts the Kings will present to the Christ Child. Other Servants may carry lanterns to light the way.

- **Wooden storage chests:** Collect large boxes with lids in a variety of sizes. Cover with brown wrapping paper and draw lines on the paper to simulate wooden planking. Depending on the size of the chests, you may wish to add rope handles.

- **Gift Boxes:** Glue plastic jewels or old costume jewelry on the gift boxes, which will be placed inside the chests. Consider covering the gift boxes in gold or silver paper or spray paint.

- **Lanterns:** Gather cylindrical, pressed-paper containers like those containing cheese snacks or chow mein noodles. Spray the outside of the container with black spray paint. Cut designs in the container with a sharp X-acto knife. Cut an X in the lid. Slip a small flashlight inside. Add a handle made out of a wire coat hanger.

- **Walking sticks:** Cut a tree branch as long as the child is tall, and trim off small branches and leaves.

- **"TAXES" signs:** Using posterboard and permanent markers, draw signs using these phrases: "NO MORE TAXES!" "READ MY LIPS! TAXES—NO!" "DOWN WITH TAXES!" "WE MAKE IT/YOU TAKE IT!"

Holding Auditions

Purpose of the Auditions

• To identify dramatic talent and potential for worship leadership
• To select persons for speaking, singing, pantomiming, movement, and instrumental roles

Materials

❑ *Leader/Accompanist Edition*
❑ *Singer's Edition*
❑ Space where auditions can be held privately
❑ One copy of the audition form for each child auditioning

Instructions for Holding Auditions

Familiarize yourself with the roles and have in mind the kind of personality needed for each character.

Let all children know ahead of time that speaking and singing roles must be memorized.

Audition children individually.

Select a passage to be used for the auditions. The opening dialogue is a possibility.

Create a familiar situation for determining ability to pantomime; for example, showing facial reactions to a surprise, fear, happiness, and so forth.

Ask each child to sing stanza 1 of "9b. What Child Is This" (*Singer's Edition*, page 17). Select strong singers for the roles of Mary and Young Joseph. The persons singing as Angels, Shepherds, Kings, and Servants will be singing in a small ensemble—these roles are perfect for the child who shows potential and needs this experience to gain confidence. If you find several good soloists during the audition process, consider using a portion of a chorus stanza as a solo.

Explain that the auditions will help in the selection of persons for the specific roles. Tell the children that while some will be assigned roles, you will also need persons to help with set design, costumes, production details, and so forth. Remind them that you will also need persons to play the Orff-style accompaniment and the camel or sleigh bells.

AUDITION FORM

NAME _____ AGE _____ GRADE _____ GENDER_____

Interested in portraying which part? _____

Sings on pitch? _____

Vocal range? _____

Projects voice? _____

Speaks clearly and slowly? _____

Physical expression/dramatics? _____

Confidence/poise? _____

Follows instructions? _____

Interested in set design, costumes, publicity? _____

Shows interest/potential as:
(*circle all possibilities*)

Chorus Member	Soloist	Speaker
Young Joseph	Old Joseph	Mary
Shepherd	Angel	King
Servant		

Stage Manager	Costume Manager
Publicity Coordinator	Percussionist
Orff instrument player	

Rehearsing a Part

Purpose of Rehearsing a Part

- To prepare the children with specific roles to deliver their lines and movement with clarity and confidence
- To enable the individual characters to come alive with dramatic emphasis and to communicate the story well

Materials

- ❏ *Leader/Accompanist Edition*
- ❏ *Singer's Edition*
- ❏ Spaces where dialogue and movement rehearsals can be held without disruption

Instructions for Rehearsing Lines and Movement

Be ready to direct line and movement rehearsals beginning with Session Four.

Know how you want speaking parts to be delivered and work toward this end. Model for the children the mental image of the characters you have in mind, but allow for personal interpretation as well.

Talk with the children about their characters. Emphasize that development of the character is just as important as learning the lines or basic movement.

Explain the words and phrases so that the children with speaking lines understand what they are saying. Describe images for the children with movement parts so they understand what pictures their bodies must communicate.

Encourage the children to practice their roles with one another at home, over the phone, in front of a mirror, and so forth.

Insist that they listen and watch one another during rehearsals with other characters. Listening to others can help them with their delivery as well.

Preparing Publicity

Purpose of Publicity

- To create congregational awareness, involvement, and anticipation
- To utilize *What Child Was This?* as an opportunity to draw inactive members or people from outside the church into congregational worship

Materials

- ❑ Supplies for making posters or other visuals (permanent markers, paint, posterboard, tape)
- ❑ A list of contact persons from local newspapers, radio and television stations, with telephone numbers and addresses
- ❑ Videotaping equipment

Instructions for Preparing the Publicity

Plan to involve the children who have volunteered to serve as Publicity Coordinators in all publicity decisions and development. Let them create and develop some of their own ideas.

Use the publicity to help create momentum and a sense of anticipation among the cast and the congregation.

In all publicity, emphasize that *What Child Was This?* will be presented as a proclamation of the Word during congregational worship.

Know the deadlines for submitting announcements to the church office for worship bulletins, newsletters, Sunday morning announcement time, and so forth. Make sure Publicity Coordinators are aware of these deadlines, and remind them as the dates draw near.

Enable the Publicity Coordinators to compose newsletter, bulletin, or newspaper publicity articles during Session Five.

Have the children work on publicity posters and so forth during Session Six.

Encourage the children to invite their friends and families as a means of witnessing to others.

Consider some of the following additional strategies:

- Contact your local newspaper to see if it is interested in publishing a picture of the children practicing. (Newspapers prefer a picture of the children actually doing something rather than standing in a line.)
  - Have some children appear in character to promote *What Child Was This?* during the Sunday school or worship announcement time.
  - Videotape a sixty-second commercial, and play it for adult Sunday school classes, Sunday morning fellowship times, or other church gatherings.
  - Have the children design bulletin inserts announcing *What Child Was This?*
- Place the palm tree from the set in a prominent place with a sign nearby advertising the musical. Have children dressed in costumes hand out fliers before and after worship one Sunday prior to the Sunday you will be presenting the musical.

Staging the Story

Purpose of Staging

• To enable the cast to maintain the flow of the presentation with intentional, natural movement

• To position characters for the most effective delivery of songs, pantomime, and spoken lines

Materials

❑ Notebook for staging notes

❑ Pen or pencil

❑ A sketch of the space where the musical is to be staged and several copies of the sketch for mapping out the movement

Instructions for Staging the Story

Read through the entire script and mark each place where there is movement of individuals, groups of characters, or the entire cast.

Using the sketches of the stage area, map out entrances, positions, on-stage movements, and exits. Having this done in advance will make your rehearsals flow much more easily.

Make sure that movements do not obscure principal characters.

Work with all cast members so that they sustain their characters at all times—even as they move from the stage area into the congregation while they sing "8. Born This Night" (Reprise) and as they disperse into the congregation.

Insist that the children remain attentive while they are learning staging so that their movements can be memorized.

Advise the children not to turn their backs to the congregation (unless required to do so in the story).

Have the movements and actions of Mary, Young Joseph, Old Joseph, Shepherds, Angels, Kings, and Servants well thought out before you begin working with them during the Session Four "Into the Drama" time.

Encourage the older children to assist the younger ones in learning the staging.

Get Moving

Purpose of the Movements
- To emphasize the text of a song
- To help set the atmosphere in a scene

Instructions for Movements

Allow plenty of time to work with the children on the movements. Make sure they rehearse the movements several times in the context of the whole song.

"2. Taxes, Taxes"

Movement is planned for the refrains. Allow the children to move freely during the stanzas.

Taxes,	taxes,	all they want are taxes.

Hold signs low.	Raise signs up slightly.	Raise signs up gradually, raising them higher with each word until the signs are above the children's heads.

"3. We've Come So Far"

When a word is underlined, the children should move as they sing that word and continue the movement until the next underlined word.

Soon a new baby will join the two;	<u>Search</u> for shelter is what they must do.	Will the fair <u>city</u>,	its gate <u>opened wide</u>	<u>Welcome</u> them warmly	<u>to dwell inside</u>?

Stand with hands at sides.	Right hand moves to left side at waist height, palm up, and slowly sweeps across body at waist height. Continue into next phrase.	Hands at chest height, palms down and fingers together; pointer fingers touching to create a "gate."	Sweep hands slowly apart and out in a circle, meeting together at the top of the circle.	Palms up.	Continue to hold hands together, palms up. Then slowly drop hands to sides.

"4. All the Sky Was Filled with Angels"

The children should move as they sing the underlined words
and continue the movement until the next underlined word.

Stanza 1:

As they had for
<u>generations</u>

Hands out, palms up at waist
height.

shepherds huddled in
the <u>cold</u>;

Rub hands together as if cold.

Telling tales of
ancient <u>longings</u>

Cross arms over chest.

that the prophets <u>had</u>
<u>foretold</u>

Leaving arms crossed, move
them up and out, pulsing on
each underlined syllable.

Stanza 2:

Then the <u>sky</u> burst
forth with singing,

Right hand shoots up
suddenly.

And the night gave up
its <u>dread</u>.

Right hand drops very slowly
through the word "dread."

<u>Angel</u> wings

Move left hand, palm down,
across body at waist height.

<u>swept</u> 'cross the
heavens,

Sweep arm up and back
across to left side of body.
Hold arm out at waist height.

lifting <u>heart</u>

Left hand to heart.

and <u>soul</u>

Right hand to heart.

and <u>head</u>.

Both hands straight up, drop with final
consonant "d."

47

"7b. Hush! Hush!"

These motions should be very gentle and smooth. Divide the choir into three groups and continue the motions through the three-part canon.

There's a baby sleeping.	**Hush! Hush!**	**Deep in slumber steeping.**	**Hush! Hush!**

Make a cradle out of arms and rock.	Place right-hand index finger in front of mouth (as if saying "shhh").	Repeat cradle-rocking motion.	Repeat "Hush!" motion.

Mary needs her rest now.	**Hush! Hush!**	**To depart is best now.**	**Hush! Hush!**

Bend head slightly and put hands together under head as though sleeping.	Repeat "Hush!" motion.	Tiptoe silently in place.	Continue tiptoeing and add "Hush!" motion.

There's a baby sleeping.	**Hush!**

Repeat "cradle" motion.	Repeat "Hush!" motion.

What Child Was This?

A Musical Story Based on Luke 2:1-20 and Matthew 2:1-2 for Unison and Two-Part Children's Voices

by John D. Horman

Setting: A small carpentry shop in which an elderly Joseph is working *(stage right)*.

Musical Selections:

1. Overture

In the tempi of the tunes within the musical

($\quarternote$ = ca. 92)

50

(**Old Joseph** *is building a small manger, putting the sides together and strengthening the legs. He uses a blunt hammer and chisel to pound the rungs into the body of the manger. He adjusts the legs to make the manger stand straight and level.* **Old Joseph** *stops working, puts down his tools, and wipes his brow with a rag that he pulls from his waistband.*)

Old Joseph: Good day, fine people! I'm glad you're here! My name is Joseph ben Jacob. I hope you don't mind if I continue my work while we talk. I'm sure you recognize what I'm making. *(He holds up a partially repaired wooden manger.)* In fact, this object brings back many memories—memories of a time long ago when the events of a special night brought together some very wonderful people. But, I'm getting ahead of myself. Let me begin at the beginning. . . .

I was engaged to a beautiful young woman named Mary. We lived in the country of Judea. Because a census was being taken, I had to return to my ancestral home to be registered and taxed. My hometown was called Bethlehem.

2. Taxes, Taxes

(Speech Chorus and Percussion)*

(The chorus is divided into four to six groups, each placed at different points in the presentation area. Members of each group hold signs that read: "NO MORE TAXES!" "READ MY LIPS! TAXES—NO!" "DOWN WITH TAXES!" "WE MAKE IT/YOU TAKE IT!" The groups move toward their risers as they speak the initial refrain.)

Use percussion instruments (such as bongos, woodblocks, and claves) to play ad lib syncopated fills throughout, especially in the two measures of rests.

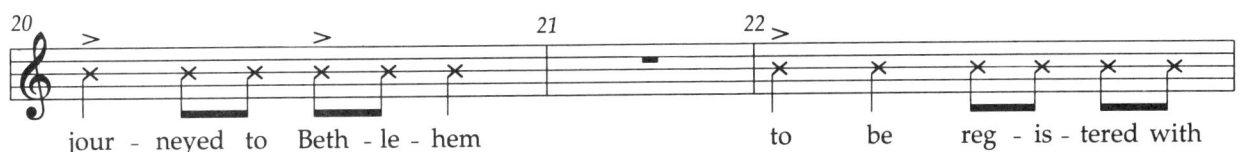

journeyed to Bethlehem to be registered with

many others and pay their taxes; pay their taxes; Pay their

Canon

Part I:

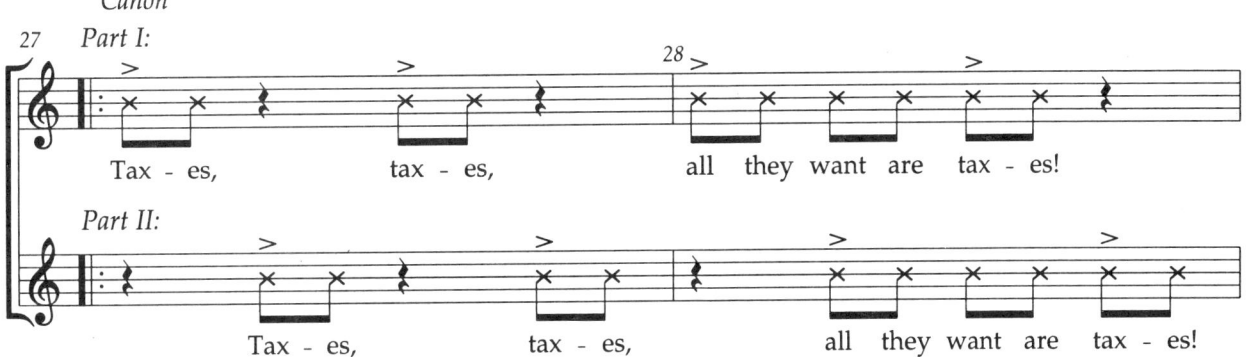

Taxes, taxes, all they want are taxes!

Part II:

Taxes, taxes, all they want are taxes!

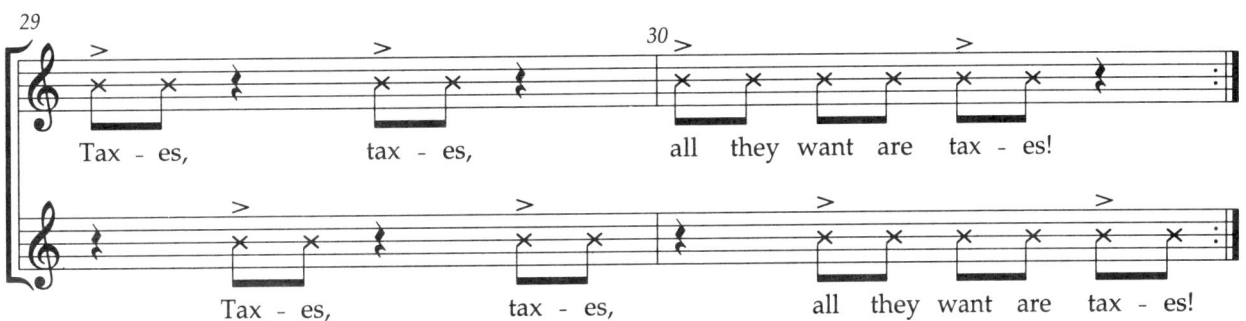

Taxes, taxes, all they want are taxes!

Taxes, taxes, all they want are taxes!

Old Joseph: Mary accompanied me on the journey to Bethlehem, over sixty miles of winding road, a journey difficult for most people to endure. It was even more difficult for Mary because she was pregnant. The days were long and the road was rough. I will never forget how Mary accepted the hardships of the journey. She never complained. She always looked confident and had an unspoken peace about her.

*(As they enter the presentation area, **Mary** and **Young Joseph** stand at the far end of the aisle leading to the stable scene.)*

Young Joseph: The trip is taking longer than I expected. It has taken us nearly a week to get here—and that's with traveling all day and into each night. I worry about you, Mary. This is not an easy trip for you to take so close to when the baby is due.

Mary: Please don't worry, Joseph. Everything will be all right. I am young and healthy. We must have faith in the power of God. All will be as our God intends.

3. We've Come So Far

(Mary, Young Joseph, and Chorus)

Bells needed:

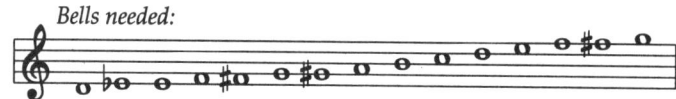

At a relaxed pace (♩ = ca. 100)

Piano

mp

poco rit.

Mary and Young Joseph:

A *mf* a tempo

1. We've come so far, both day and night.
2. Long is the road; it twists up and down.

mf a tempo

f

On - ly the stars to give us light.
O - ver that hill sure - ly Beth - le - hem's found.

f

Braving the perils that lie in our way,
Though we're unsure what the future may hold,

closer to Bethlehem every day.
faith in the power of God keeps us whole.

With more motion

B 1st time - Young Joseph
2nd time - Mary

Mary grows tired, weary, and worn.
Sweet is my Joseph, he walks by my side.

Soon a new ba - by to us will be born.
Though ex - haust - ed, he makes me ride.

Soon a new ba - by will join the two;

search for shel - ter is what they must do.

56

Will the fair cit - y, its gates o - pened wide,

wel - come them warm - ly to dwell in - side?

D *More motion*

Young Joseph: **mf**

Look! In the dis - tance, the town is in view

where Jo - seph's fam - i - ly lived and grew.

Tired are we; soon to be three.

On our way, on their way, on the

way to Beth - le - hem.

(**Young Joseph** *and* **Mary** *make their way down the center aisle of the church during this song.*)

    Old Joseph: As we approached the town, we noticed shepherds faithfully tending their sheep on the surrounding hillsides. We envied the shepherds' quiet and simple lives. Little did we know that their lives were about to be turned upside down, and that the baby soon to be born would be the cause of the uproar.

(**Mary** *and* **Young Joseph** *continue into Bethlehem, stopping at individual chorus members to ask for shelter. Each one shakes his or her head and turns his or her back until finally one person takes the couple to a stable at centerstage.* **Shepherds** *are gathered on the lower part of a hillside made of a covered riser, stage left. They point to the sky and excitedly describe what they see.*)

    Shepherd 1: Look! What's that in the sky?

Shepherd 2: Lights! Bright, glowing lights and angels! Oh, look! So many angels!

(The **Shepherds** *react with fear by kneeling and covering their heads with their hands and arms.* **Angels** *appear on the top of the riser.)*

Angel 1: Do not be afraid! We bring you good news of great joy for all people everywhere!

Angel 2: Born to you this night in the City of David is a Savior who is Christ, the Lord!

Shepherd 3: *(To the other shepherds)* Listen! Do you hear those sounds? The angels are singing! It's so beautiful!

*(***Angels*** may sing a portion or all of stanza 4 of "All the Sky Was Filled with Angels." See letter B in the musical score.)*

4. All the Sky Was Filled with Angels

(Chorus, Shepherds, and Angels)

Bells needed:

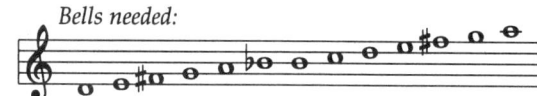

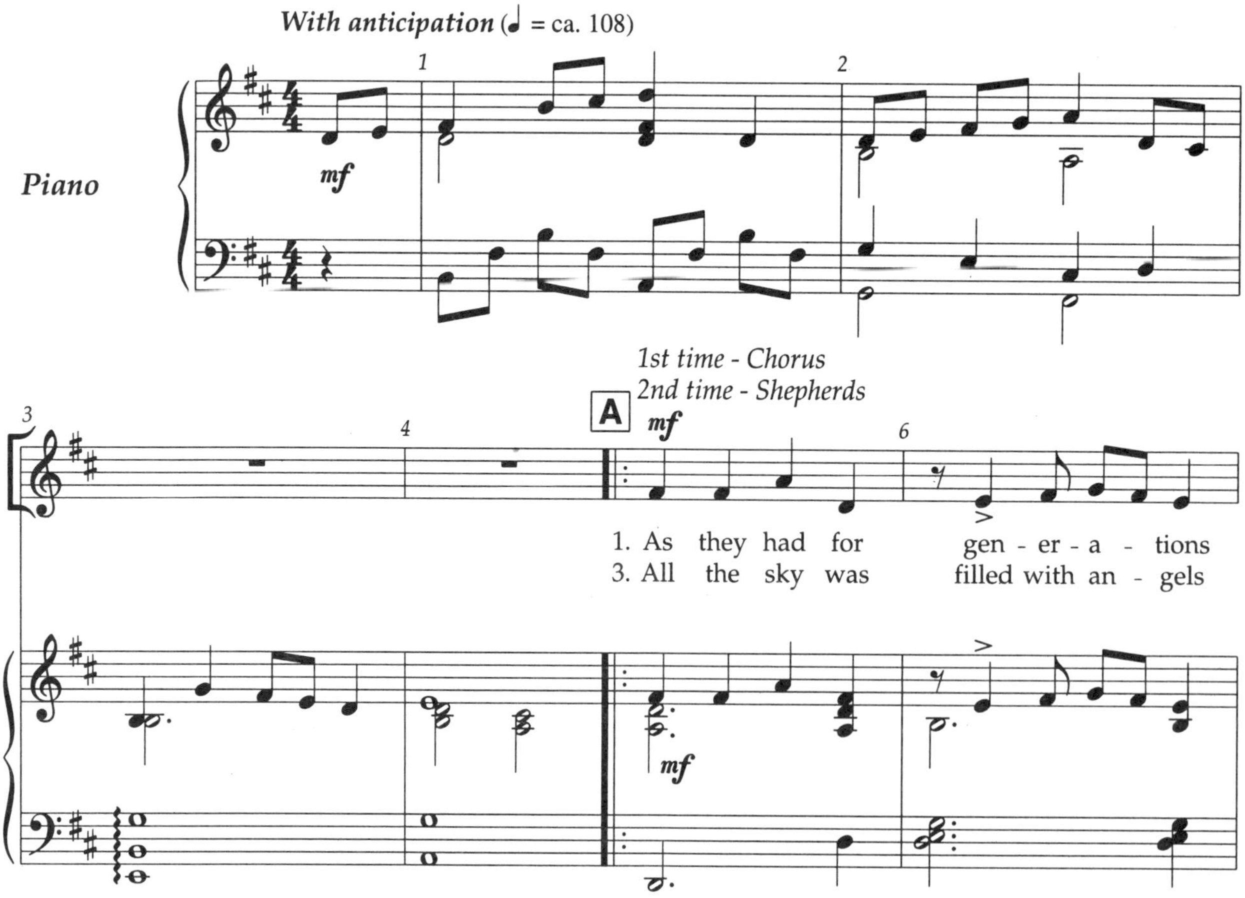

With anticipation (♩ = ca. 108)
Piano
mf
1st time - Chorus
2nd time - Shepherds
A
1. As they had for gen - er - a - tions
3. All the sky was filled with an - gels

*Flute may double top line in measures 13-16.

An-gel wings swept 'cross the heav - ens, lift-ing
Glo-ry, glo-ry in the high - est! Tid-ings

heart and soul and head.
of great joy we bring."

*Flute may double top line in measures 26-29.

rall.

(musical notation, measures 35-37)

high - est! Tid-ings of great joy we bring."

heaven - ly an - gels sing - ing of a new - born boy.

*(Following the song, the **Shepherds** and **Angels** move to the stable area and gather around the manger.)*

Old Joseph: The shepherds were very excited when they found us. They had seen a multitude of the heavenly host filling the night sky with song. It must have been quite a sight indeed! Mary and I understood their excitement, for we had once been visited by an angel ourselves. By the time the shepherds arrived at the stable, Mary had already given birth to our baby. She lovingly cradled him in her arms for all to see.

Young Joseph: What shall we name him?

Mary: We will call him "Jesus."

5. Born This Night

(Chorus and Shepherd Soloist)

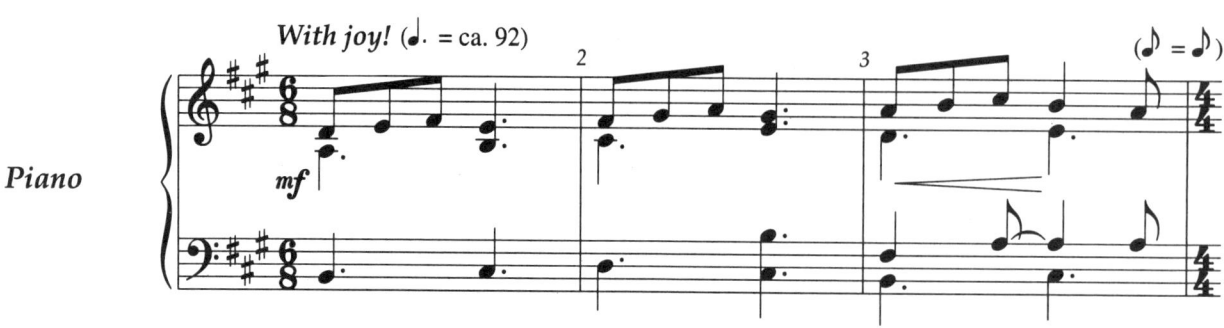

Tambourine: A

Chorus: f

Born this night a ba - by small. Born this night to save us all!

Peace and joy to us he brings. Lift your voice! Lift your voice!

65

Lift your voice, and come with us. Sing! _____

rit. **B** *Slightly slower*

rit. Shepherd Solo: *mf*

God is sure - ly here this night,

bathed in glo - ry, clothed in light. He who came for

us to-day lies in slum-ber on the hay.

Tempo I
C Flute:
mf

Tempo I
Tambourine:
f

Tempo I
Chorus:
f
Born this night a ba - by small. Born this night to

Tempo I
f

save us all! Peace and joy to us he brings.

Lift your voice! Lift your voice! Lift your voice, and

come with us. Sing!

(**Shepherds** and **Angels** *leave the stable area immediately following the song.* **Angels** *may join the choir or exit, and the* **Shepherds** *return to their flocks on the hillside, stage left.*)

Old Joseph: Yes, he was called "Jesus," which means "Jehovah's salvation." Mary and I remained in Bethlehem, loving our son and watching him grow. He filled our lives with joy as we went about our daily routine. We had no idea that more visitors were on the way. In fact, a splendid procession was already approaching from the East.

6. Procession of the Kings*
(Instrumental)

Drums and camel or sleigh bells may be added as they seem appropriate.

*(Processing down an aisle of the church, **Kings** and **Servants** arrive. They march slowly, accompanied by the sound of camel bells and the music to "Procession of the Kings.")*

King 1: We must hurry!

King 2: *(He cups a hand to one ear to help him hear better.)* We must what?

King 3: *(Speaking loudly to **King 2**)* We must hurry! Hurry! HURRY!

King 1: We are late!

King 2: *(With a hand cupping one ear)* We must wait?

King 3: *(Speaking louder to **King 2**)* No, we're late! Late! LATE!

King 1: He is born!

King 2: *(With a hand cupping one ear)* What is torn?

King 3: *(Speaking even louder to **King 2**, who hears him this time)* No, he is born! Born! BORN!

All Three Kings: This is he who has been born King of the Jews. We have seen his star in the East and have come to worship him.

*(The **Shepherds** see the procession and leave their flocks. They are pointing, gesturing, and talking to one another as they curiously follow the three **Kings** at a distance. After the **Kings** and **Servants** have reached the house of **Mary** and **Young Joseph**, they place their gifts before the child. The **Kings**, **Servants**, and **Shepherds** kneel together and begin talking to and questioning one another. The discussion grows louder and louder until finally **Young Joseph** speaks.)*

Young Joseph: Friends! Friends! Please hush! Your excitement will wake the child! It is very late, and Mary and the child must rest now. You need to be quiet!

*(**Young Joseph** beckons and gestures to quiet the crowd of unexpected visitors. He sings to the group.)*

7a. Hush! Hush!

(Young Joseph)

There's a ba - by sleep - ing. Hush! Hush! Deep in

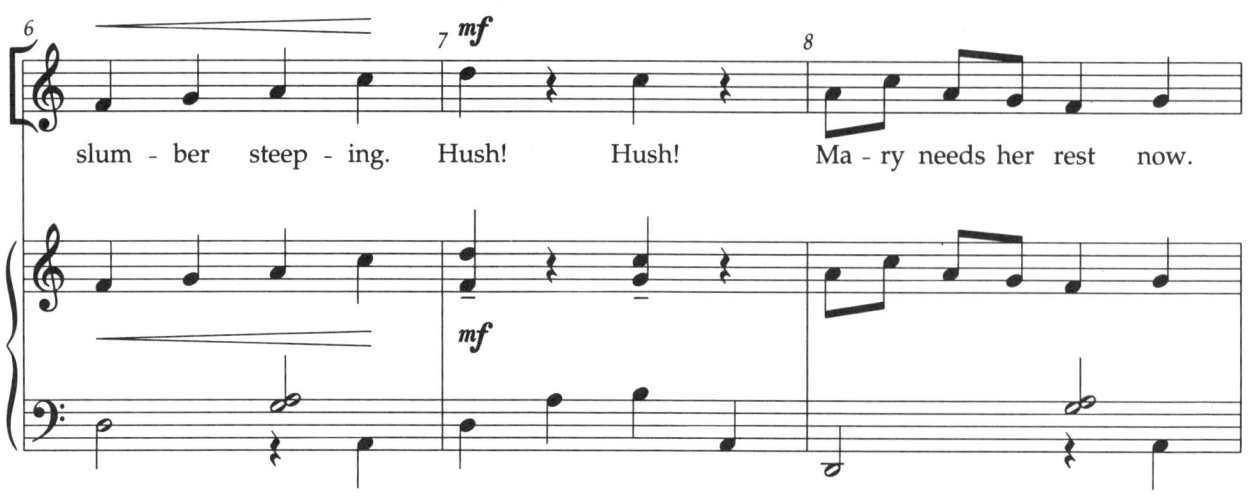

slum - ber steep - ing. Hush! Hush! Ma - ry needs her rest now.

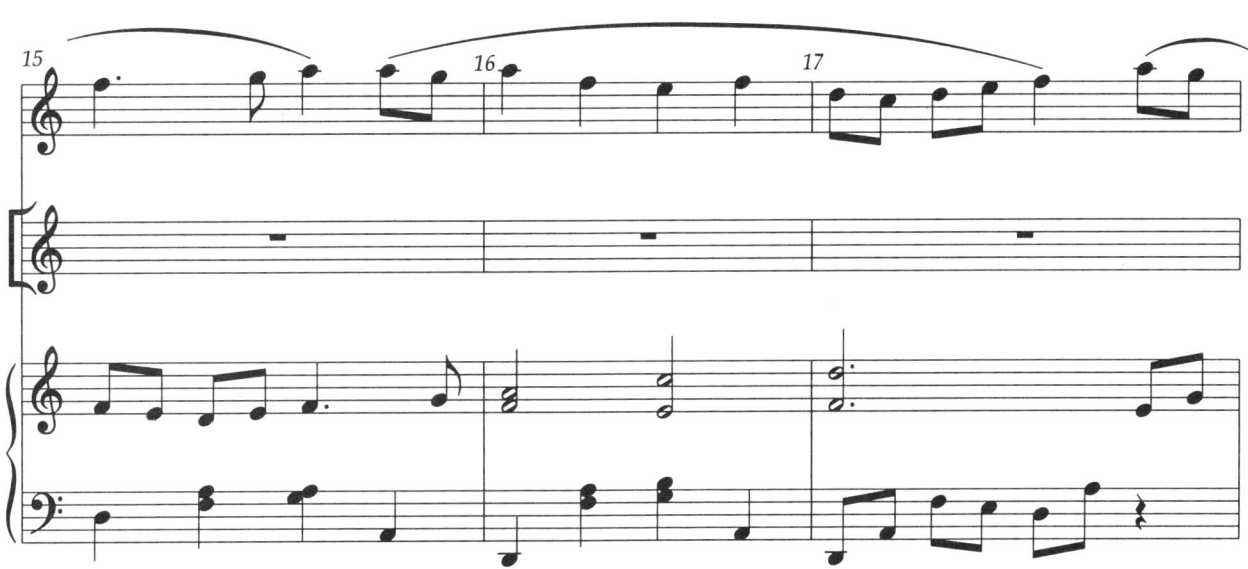

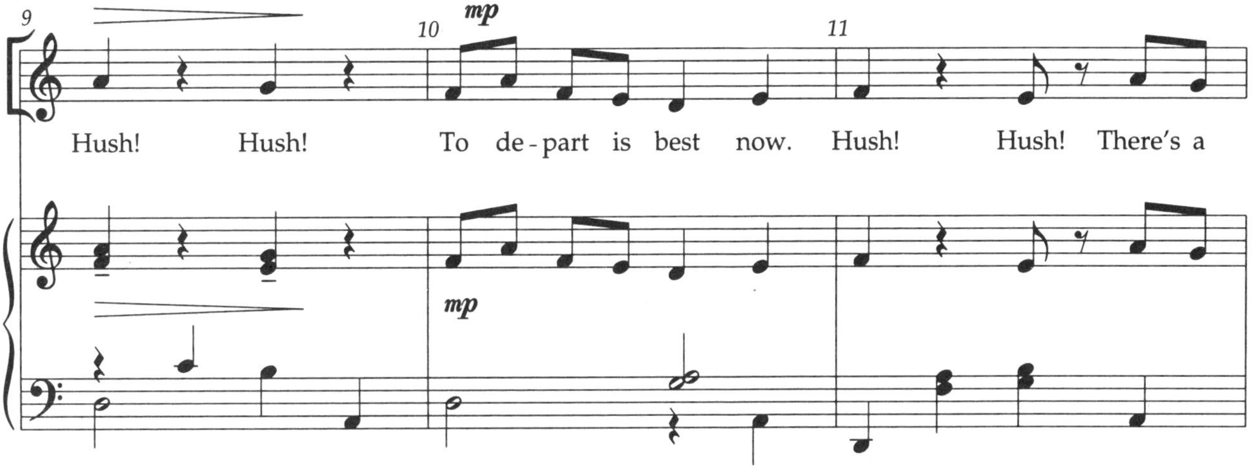
mp
Hush! Hush! To de-part is best now. Hush! Hush! There's a
mp

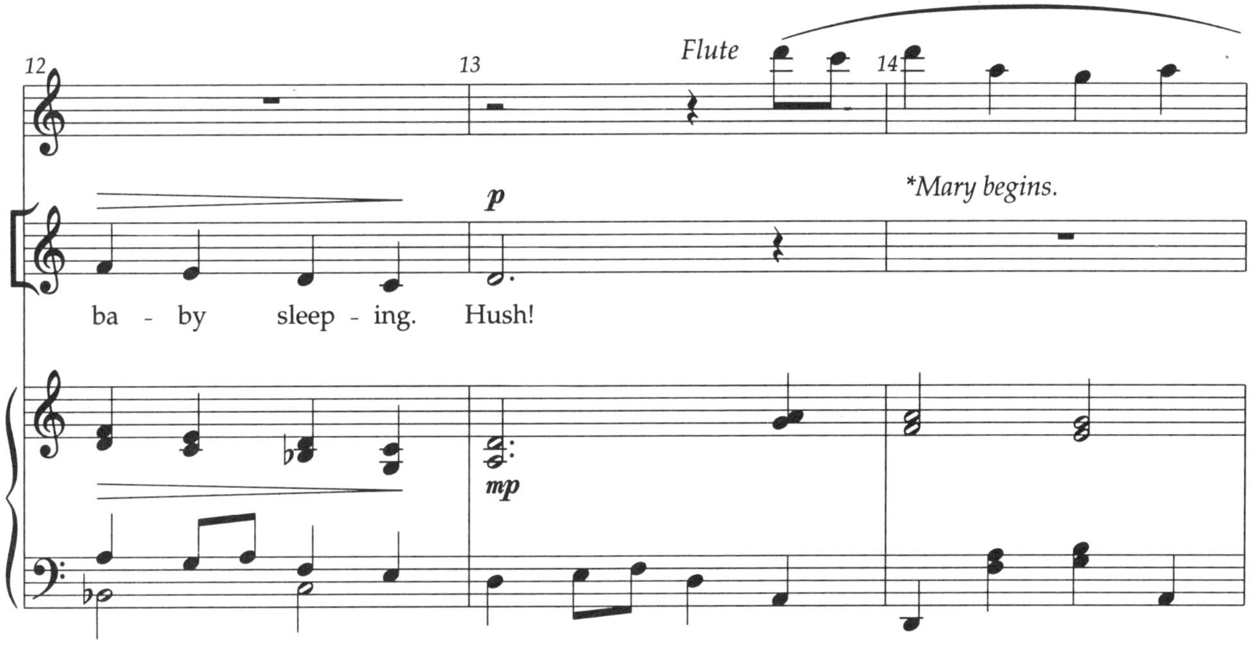
Flute
*Mary begins.
p
ba - by sleep - ing. Hush!
mp

*Mary: Thank you all! I am so glad you came. It has meant so much to me, to Joseph, and to our son. God's blessing be upon each one of you!

Young Joseph: God has led you to this place. We know that you have been chosen to be part of this most wonderful event. Would you like to see the child again? *(The* **Kings,** **Shepherds,** *and* **Servants** *nod in agreement.)* Come, but very quietly. *(***Young Joseph** *leads the group toward the child.)* See, Jesus has already fallen asleep.

7b. Hush! Hush!

(Shepherds, Kings, Servants, and Chorus)

*Orff accompaniment begins in measure 2.

(Ensemble sings in canon as it files past the baby)

* Part I could be sung by Kings, Part II by Servants, and Part III by Shepherds. Divide the choir according to how the singers will be standing.

78

*All parts put "sh" on at the same time.

79

7b. Hush! Hush!

(Orff Style Accompaniment)

Accompaniment begins on the downbeat of measure 2. To end, return to the first beat of the Orff Style Accompaniment and fermata.

© 1996 by Abingdon Press

(When the canon part of "7b. Hush! Hush!" begins, the entourage quietly files past the baby and tiptoes out of the stable area. They move toward a point in the distance as they sing. During the transition of "8. Born This Night," the **Shepherds**, **Servants**, and **Kings** reach this point, and they sing the refrain of "8. Born This Night," joined by the chorus.)

8. Born This Night (Reprise)

(Cast and Chorus)

Born this night a ba - by small.

Born this night to save us all! Peace and joy to us he brings. Lift your voice! Lift your voice!

Lift your voice, and come with us. Sing!

(*Old Joseph* leaves his workbench, carrying the manger he has been making. He walks to **Mary** and **Young Joseph** and places the manger between them. **Mary** gently lays the baby in the manger and smiles.)

> **Mary:** He will be called the Prince of Peace.

Young Joseph: "Emmanuel! God with us!"

(**Old Joseph** *faces the audience. A single flute plays "9a. What Child Is This" as he asks the following question.*)

> **Old Joseph:** "What Child was this, who born that night, deserved such adoration? What Child was this, God's gift of grace, who brought to us salvation?"

9a. What Child Is This

(Flute)

9b. What Child Is This

(Cast, Chorus, and Congregation)

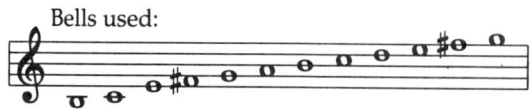

Stanza 1, 2, & 3 William Dix
Stanza 4 John Horman

16th cent. English melody
Tune: GREENSLEEVES

Flute: (play on stanzas 1, 3, and 4)

1. What child is this who laid to rest on
(2. Why) lies he in such mean es - tate where
(3. So) bring him in - cense, gold, and myrrh, come,
(4. What) child was this, who born that night, de -

Ma - ry's lap is sleep - ing? Whom an - gels greet with
ox and ass are feed - ing? Good Chris - tians, fear, for
peas - ant, king, to own him; the King of kings sal -
served such ad - o - ra - tion? What child was this, God's

an - thems sweet while shep - herds watch are keep - ing?
sin - ners here the si - lent Word is plead - ing.
va - tion brings, let lov - ing hearts en - throne him.
gift of grace, who brought to us sal - va - tion?

Handbells: (stanza 4 only)
Refrain

Refrain

Refrain

This, this is Christ the King, whom shep - herds guard and

Refrain

86

Bulletin Insert

What Child Is This

Stanzas 1, 2, 3, and refrain by William C. Dix (1865)
Stanza 4 by John Horman

1. What child is this who, laid to rest,
   On Mary's lap is sleeping?
   Whom angels greet with anthems sweet,
   While shepherds watch are keeping?

   REFRAIN: This, this is Christ the King,
   Whom shepherds guard and angels sing;
   Haste, haste to bring him laud,
   The babe, the son of Mary.

2. Why lies he in such mean estate
   Where ox and ass are feeding?
   Good Christians, fear,
   For sinners here the silent Word is pleading.

   REFRAIN

3. So bring him incense, gold, and myrrh,
   Come, peasant, king, to own him;
   The King of kings salvation brings,
   Let loving hearts enthrone him.

   REFRAIN

4. What child was this, who born that night,
   Deserved such adoration?
   What child was this, God's gift of grace,
   Who brought to us salvation?

   REFRAIN